PRAI!

"This is the new bible for crafting stories of espionage. It's also perfect for anyone who wants to know the lengths nations will go to keep or steal secrets and the methods they will use to do so. This is a bombshell of a book."

—James Rollins, *New York Times* bestseller of *The Demon Crown*

"From novices to experts, I suspect everyone will find something in this book that they did not know before."

—Doug Patteson, Film Technical Advisor and Former CIA Officer

"Detailed, insightful, and authentic, *Spycraft: Essentials* is my go-to reference for all things espionage."

—Grant Blackwood, *New York Times* bestseller of the Briggs Tanner series

"Solid, valuable information as a comprehensive primer on how the Intelligence Community really operates, *Spycraft: Essentials* is a must-read for all involved Americans. —Rob DuBois, Retired US Navy SEAL and NSA Collector

"An essential addition to every thriller writer's library. Piper Bayard and Jay Holmes know their stuff!"

—Diane Capri, *New York Times* and *USA Today* Bestseller of the Hunt for Jack Reacher series

ABOUT THE AUTHORS

Piper Bayard is an author and a recovering attorney. She is also a belly dancer, a mom, and a former hospice volunteer. She currently pens spy thrillers with Jay Holmes, as well as her own post-apocalyptic science fiction.

Jay Holmes is a forty-five year veteran of field intelligence operations spanning from the Cold War fight against the Soviets, the East Germans, and the terrorist organizations they sponsored to the present Global War on Terror. Piper is the public face of their partnership.

Together, Bayard & Holmes author nonfiction articles and books on espionage and foreign affairs, as well as fictional spy thrillers. They are the bestselling authors of *The Spy Bride* from the Risky Brides Bestsellers Collection.

When they aren't writing or, in Jay's case, busy with "other work," Piper and Jay are enjoying their families, hiking, exploring, talking foreign affairs, laughing at their own rude jokes, and questing for the perfect chocolate cake recipe. If you think you have that recipe, please share it with them at their email below.

To receive notices of upcoming Bayard & Holmes releases, subscribe to the Bayard & Holmes Covert Briefing. You can contact Bayard & Holmes at their website BayardandHolmes.com, at @piperbayard on Twitter, or at their email, BayardandHolmes@protonmail.com.

ALSO BY BAYARD & HOLMES

NONFICTION

Key Figures in Espionage

Key Moments in Espionage

Timeline Iran: Stone Age to Nuclear Age

MORE SPYCRAFT COMING SOON

Key People and Wars

FICTION BY BAYARD & HOLMES

The Spy Bride

Apex Predator Series Coming Soon

The Panther of Baracoa

The Leopard of Cairo

The Caiman of Iquitos

FICTION BY PIPER BAYARD

Firelands

SPYCRAFT: ESSENTIALS

BAYARD & HOLMES

SPYCRAFT I

Shoe Phone Press
2770 Arapahoe Road #135-229
Lafayette, CO 80026

Copyright © 2018 by Piper Bayard & Jay Holmes

Published in the United States of America.

All rights reserved as permitted under the U.S. Copyright Act of 1976. No portion of this publication may be reproduced in any form or by any electronic or mechanical means, including information storage and retrieval systems, without written permission from the authors, with the exception of reviewers, who may quote brief passages in a book review.

*For all the unsung heroes in the clandestine services—
operatives might make movies, but you make history—
and to the writers who would honor them faithfully.*

CONTENTS

Introduction	xi
1. Terminology and the Word "Spook"	1
2. The Spook Reality	7
3. The Spook Character	14
4. Spook Recruitment	21
5. Spook Training, a.k.a. Tradecraft	26
6. The Role Of Women In Espionage	28
7. Fifty Shades Of "Covert"	34
8. Special Message For Publishers	49
9. Intelligence Agencies—What, To Whom, And Where?	55
10. Electronic Surveillance	105
11. Physical Surveillance	124
12. Bugging Spaces	135
13. Finding Bugs	149
14. Essential Spook Gadgets	153
15. Espionage Myths	155
16. Honeypots And The Honeypot Assassin	185
17. Conspiracies	192
18. Sleeper Agents	198
19. Firearms Of Spycraft	203
20. Silencers	214
21. Where To Shoot The Target	221
22. Covert Communications	224
23. Poisons	229
24. Weaponized Gadgets	235
25. Truth Serums And Enhanced Interrogations	237
26. Central America and the School of the Americas	241
27. When Good Missions Go Bad—The Exit Strategy	256
28. The Hardest Part Of The Mission	259
29. What Will Be The Next Hot Spot?	262
30. The Greatest Myth	263

In Conclusion	265
Photo Gallery	267
Key Figures in Espionage	269
Acknowledgments	271

INTRODUCTION

Welcome to *Spycraft: Essentials*. This book came about when Piper taught a class in Spycraft Essentials at the Rocky Mountain Fiction Writers Colorado Gold Conference. So many of our readers who were not able to make it to the conference asked us for the information that we offered to write this reference book.

Let's be clear up front. If you're looking for a "tell-all" book of our nation's deepest, darkest espionage secrets, this is not the book for you. We are not Snowden, Manning, or Assange, nor are we part of an Intelligence Community ("IC") public relations project. While we may include an anecdote or two, what you will *not* find in this book is classified information, bragging about manhunts, details of current or recent field operations, or boasts about Holmes being the greatest spymaster the world has ever known. If you want that, you'll need to find a former junior intelligence analyst with a book contract or a Hollywood producer who once had a drink with the Navy SEAL who was dating his sister. We are simply loyal Americans working on an independent civilian project in the interest of serving the public and, in particular, writers.

Also, in real life, no one is qualified to write a tell-all book about espionage anyway. Even the Director of the Central Intelligence Agency ("CIA") is not qualified to write that book. That's because espionage, by its very nature, is compartmentalized so that no one person has the information to "tell all" about any agency or even any aspect of intelligence work. Great societal myths have been planted and have bloomed into accepted history because operatives who knew *some* thing assumed they knew *every* thing. Which leads us to our first Spycraft Essential...

Greatest Espionage Mistake: The greatest yet most common mistake an operative or any other human being can make is to think that because they know something, they know everything.

It's worth saying again. The greatest yet most common mistake an operative or any other human being can make is to think that because they know something, they know everything. In espionage, this hubris can and does have tragic consequences.

Another reason there is no such thing as a tell-all book is because the world of espionage is vast and ever changing, with every player adjusting creatively to stay ahead of the enemy. Methods evolve over the years, and politics change with each administration. As a result, one of the few constants in espionage is change.

While it's natural to all humans to want concrete, reliable answers, those who live and work in the Shadow World don't often have that luxury, and they must be prepared to expect change. If the IC didn't adapt and change, it would be utterly useless. Every operative is different, and every situation is different. Two operatives can begin on the same day, stay in the clandestine services for thirty years, and each retire having had completely different experiences. As a result, there is no such thing as a tell-all book about espionage.

What we *do* provide in this book is solid, objective information about various aspects of the personalities and personal challenges of those in espionage, the functions and jurisdictions of the main civilian intelligence organizations, common fabrications perpetuated in fiction, a bit of espionage history, information on firearms and silencers, the scoop on honeypots and sleeper agents, some hands-on espionage techniques, and the voice of almost half a century of experience in the field.

We also include writing tips for writers to employ in thier craft, but don't be fooled by that fact. This book isn't only for writers. The information contained in these pages is the straight skinny for anyone interested in learning more about American espionage.

The paramilitary element of espionage is only one small part of the intelligence picture, but it is the part that is most often portrayed in fiction; therefore, much of this book addresses fieldwork and operatives. However, thousands of hardworking analysts, programmers, scientists, engineers, agent handlers, educators, recruiters, trainers, couriers, lawyers, linguists, janitors, etc., play roles that are just as vital to national security. Every job in the IC is important, and everyone who serves in the IC contributes to the safety of our nation. Our deepest gratitude to these excellent intelligence professionals.

So who are we to write this book?

Rather than dazzle you with bullshit, we will state our credentials simply: Piper is an author and a recovering attorney who has worked daily with Holmes for the past decade, learning about foreign affairs, espionage history, and field techniques for the purpose of writing both fiction and nonfiction. Holmes is a forty-five-year veteran of field espionage operations. Since Holmes is still covert, Piper is the public face of their partnership. We'll get into the why of that more in the chapter about what constitutes "covert."

Why are we writing this book?

Because we're getting really tired of walking out of movies and throwing books against the wall. Because we're not the kind of people to complain about something without trying to make it better. Because we're hoping you'll give us money in exchange for our efforts and experience. We see it as a win/win. The public gets an education, the world of fiction gets a bit less fictitious, and we get to support our habit of sharing factual information about the Shadow World we love.

1
TERMINOLOGY AND THE WORD "SPOOK"

VOCABULARY, LIKE THE ORGANIZATIONAL CHART, IS EVER-EVOLVING and shifts decade by decade. However, some terms are general and widespread enough to be enduring. So a little vocabulary to begin with, just so we're all on the same page...

SPY vs. SPOOK

As we mention above, Holmes is a forty-something-year veteran of the Intelligence Community. Is Holmes a spy? No. Holmes is a "spook."

"Spying is seamy. It's what the Russians do." ~ Jay Holmes

There are two instances in the IC when "spy" is the appropriate term. First, it is used when referring to individuals involved in espionage against us. Second, the term "spy" is used to refer to foreign agents we recruit to "spy" for us against their own nation or organization. It is generally not used in the Intelligence

Community to apply to our own espionage operatives and officers.

The preferred slang among American intelligence officers and operatives and in the IC in general is "spook," not "spy." It's a common, age-old nickname that will not be found in any training syllabus. The word "spook" usually is not used by spooks to describe themselves so much as it is used to describe other groups of spooks. For example, Department of Homeland Security ("DHS") agents might say something like, "We have a meeting with the spooks at 3:00 p.m.," meaning they have a meeting with the CIA.

Usage of the term "spook" in the Intelligence Community dates back to the 1800s and is derived from "a ghost that haunts people and is considered undesirable." It has nothing to do with the racial slur, and operatives of all races are referred to as "spooks."

Each organization might also have its specific terminology to refer to its officers and operatives. For example, CIA officers, particularly the younger ones, currently refer to themselves and each other as "OOs" and "COs," meaning Operations Officers and Case Officers, respectively. However, the term "spook" is more of a blanket term that loosely applies to everyone in the IC at large from US Navy cryptologic technicians to CIA analysts at Headquarters.

The military also commonly refers to both its own intelligence operatives and civilian intelligence operatives as "spooks." Some folks at the DHS apply the term "spook" to themselves, as well; however, everyone else in the IC outside of DHS pretty much calls them "those guys at DHS."

The exception to the use of the term "spook" in the IC is the Federal Bureau of Investigation ("FBI"). FBI agents do not see themselves as spooks. That's likely because their primary mission is collecting evidence for the sake of criminal prosecution rather than collecting it as part of intelligence gathering. This emphasis on criminal prosecution impacts the mindset and overall mentality of the FBI. They refer to themselves as "FBI agents" rather than "spooks."

Since some people may not be familiar or comfortable with the usage of the term "spook" as anything but a racial slur, we'll provide examples to encourage folks to relax with it.

Examples:

"I worked as a spook for the NSA for ten years."

"This old spook prefers cruise missiles to hand-to-hand combat."

"Holmes, you'd be amazed at how many spooks are on Twitter."

"¡Carajo! What the hell are spooks doing on Twitter?" (Holmes being amazed when Piper told him about the spooks she met on Twitter.)

Spooks often trek about the globe on military transports. When a spook or a group of spooks is on a military ship or a submarine, the regular military personnel refer to them as "the spooks."

Example:

"Wow! She's really hot."

"Yeah. Watch out. She's one of the spooks."

When writing fiction, some characters, particularly the younger ones, might prefer specific agency terminology to the slang "spook." Please don't resort to the word "spy." Instead, consult someone in the character's specific organization and find out what the terminology is for that organization. This can be done by calling the organization's contact number at their web site. To find the web site, search on "[Organization Name] public contact number."

> **Side Note:** As a general rule, spooks and regular military personnel on ships don't socialize with each other. This is largely for security reasons.

> **Bottom Line:** Remember that the good guys are "spooks," not "spies." "Spies" are Russians, Iranians, North Koreans, and other such unscrupulous foreign agents who work against us. "Spies" are also foreigners who work *for* us against their own nation or organization.

> **Writing Tip:** Some authors still might be shy about using the word "spook." We encourage you to not surrender authenticity, but rather to lightly pepper the word "spook" in contexts where the meaning is clear and it cannot be mistaken for the racial slur, especially with older IC characters. Let's help keep the public educated about vocabulary. There are enough racial slurs for bigots to choose from. They can't have this one.

OPERATIVE vs. OFFICER vs. AGENT

The more technical terms for spooks are "operatives," "officers," and "agents."

The term "operative" can apply to both CIA employees and contractors, as well as to spooks from other civilian and military intelligence organizations. It is a vague term that mostly refers to men and women in the field, but it has no hard and fast definition. By habit, when CIA operatives are talking amongst themselves more formally or when they are reviewing an operation, they refer to themselves as "operatives."

"Officer" is a term particular to the CIA. CIA operations officers are employees, not contractors. Generally, they work at Headquarters or under diplomatic cover and are the individuals who spot, assess, develop, recruit, and handle the people that collect and transmit foreign intelligence. Though the terms "operative" and "officer" can overlap in their application, as a general rule, operations officers are not referred to as "operatives," and many bristle at the word. Some officers dislike being called "operatives" because they believe the term "operative" feels a bit too "Hollywood." Other officers dislike being called "operatives" because operatives are largely considered to be a bit shady by the more mainstream elements of the IC.

Intelligence "agents," on the other hand, are almost always foreigners that collect information in foreign countries and deliver it to the intelligence operatives and officers. In other words, the "operatives" and "officers" are the intelligence personnel who manage the "foreign agents." So technically, the classic song "Secret Agent Man" should really be "Secret Operative Man" or "Secret Officer Man."

The CIA uses the word "agent" in a very specific way. Other intelligence organizations use the term "agent" in different ways. For example, the FBI, Secret Service, and DHS employees carry badges that say "agent" on them. In that context, the term "agent" implies law enforcement power and formal prosecution. "Operatives," on the other hand, are generally not about prosecution, but rather about collecting information for power management or terrorism prevention, analyzing information collected and passing it on, or blowing things up. We'll discuss more about which agencies have law enforcement powers in a later chapter.

Bottom Line: Intelligence "operatives" are employees and contractors that generally, but not always, work in the field. The term is vague. "Officers" are specifically CIA employees, and they spot, assess, develop, recruit, and handle "agents." Intelligence "agents" in the context of the CIA are foreigners who report to "operatives" and "officers." "Agent" is also a term used for employees of the FBI, the DHS, the Secret Service, and some other military and civilian intelligence branches.

2
THE SPOOK REALITY

THE INTELLIGENCE COMMUNITY IS VAST AND VARIED. SOME SPOOKS lead relatively normal lives in relatively safe environments, commuting to work at an office and watching their children's soccer games. Some spooks live in the United States and some live abroad. Some of those who live abroad lead a relatively normal existence, such as spooks who work in embassies and other government installations. Others are abroad working under covers or "legends," which we discuss at length later in this book. Some spooks are in allied nations, and some are in "denied areas," which are hostile nations such as Russia, China, Iran, or any other country whose basic interests and political aspirations are at odds with the United States. Still others live and work in the United States and are assigned periodically for missions that may last from a day to several months or, in rare cases, two or three years. There is no one pattern for a "spook life," and the same spook might experience any number of these lifestyles during the course of their career.

Fiction, however, has most of its fun with the field spooks. The terms "field spook" and "field operative" are rather generic and imprecise and not to be found in *Merriam-Webster*. As a general rule, they refer to spooks who travel abroad and operate outside of official government facilities.

> *"Every field spook has two personalities—the one they have at home and the one they have on the mission."* ~ Jay Holmes

THE FIELD SPOOK AT HOME

A field spook can have any personality at home. They can be somber or lighthearted. They can be wealthy or living with one foot on the street and the other on a banana peel. They can be dog lovers, PTA presidents, LGBT advocates, or eco-warriors. They can be quirky or straightlaced. They can be promiscuous, monks, single, divorced, or family people. They can be West Point graduates, Marine grunts, or Harvard language specialists. They can be Democrats, Republicans, Libertarians, etc., or they can eschew politics altogether. They can be Christians, Jews, Muslims, Wiccans, Atheists, or any other religious flavor. They might spend their days in wild and exciting pursuits, or they might fill their hours between missions doing laundry and walking behind their children turning off lights.

> **Writing Tip:** As a writer, let your imagination cut loose with the field spook personality at home. There is no "right" way to be an off-duty spook, so long as that character is consistent with the core character traits of spooks as covered in The Spook Character section of this book.

How much a field spook can tell their spouse about their employment can vary. For example, a CIA officer who works under Diplomatic Cover (See Fifty Shades of "Covert") may be required to tell their spouse they work for the CIA. Such an officer might even employ their spouse's assistance in spotting, assessing, and developing assets. However, some covert spooks in other areas of the IC, such as those who are part of Special Access Programs (See Fifty Shades of "Covert"), will not even be able to tell their spouses exactly what program they are in, much less anything about the nature of that work.

In the latter situation, spouses and children might know their loved one works for the government, and families will see that sometimes their loved one seems a bit stressed for reasons that cannot be divulged. A spook's family may also be aware that their loved one will be in danger while they're gone, but the family won't know anything about the specifics. The spook will get a phone call and tell their loved ones something like, "I need to pack and leave tonight. It shouldn't be for too long," or "I need to leave for a while. I don't know how long." The spook may or may not be able to leave an emergency contact number with their spouse and children. Often this will be all that families ever know of their loved one's work.

This is for two reasons. First, it is to protect the families. If our enemies know that this variety of US field spook never tells their families any information, our enemies won't bother to kidnap our spooks' families to torture them. Second, it is to protect our spooks and the Intelligence Community. It's a challenging lifestyle, and many relationships don't survive it. A vindictive former spouse could cause a severe security breach if they know anything important. The exception to this would be when the spook is going undercover for a long term, such as two or three years. At that point, they can't just disappear without telling their spouse *something*. In such cases, though, a spook would still only tell their spouse the bare minimum.

Being married to a field spook who is constantly disappearing to parts unknown for undetermined time periods can be hard on a marriage, and as with any situation, the survival of the union depends upon the nature of the relationship. Some marriages are destined to self-destruct and some endure the most difficult trials. Most fall somewhere in between, with committed people who are torn by life's changes and challenges. However, because the lifestyle of the absent-without-a-trace type of field spook *is* so difficult, there is a higher incidence of spooks staying single, being divorced, or being married without children. Some spooks say the most successful spook marriages are those where both partners are spooks, and some say the most successful spook marriages are those without children where the spouse also has a demanding career, lending more tolerance for the spook's absences and dedication to their work. Much depends on the personalities and the stresses the spook's work puts on the union.

Children are also deeply impacted by the sudden and prolonged absences of their field spook parent. As with any situation where a parent is frequently absent, the children's development and emotional well-being can suffer. There's no getting around that. This can be made more intense because the field spook often can't call home or Skype, and they can't be open with their children about where they are or what they're doing. Such a dynamic can cause emotional scars and feelings of abandonment that can plague the children long after they are old enough to understand their spook parent's calling. This is one of the many sacrifices the entire family makes when their family member serves in the clandestine services.

Friendships can be difficult to maintain as well. A spook may hang out with someone every few days or every week, entertain them as a houseguest, go hiking together, share dinners, commiserate about their HOA boards, and engage in other bonding activities, only to randomly disappear for various periods of time with no warning. This frequently leaves friends bewildered, wondering what happened and whether the spook is actually a friend at all. When the spook shows up again, friends are expected to accept their sudden disappearance and reappearance with no explanation. Not every friendship can roll with that, even if the friends guess accurately that the person is part of the IC. Close friendships need a certain amount of reliability to thrive, and that isn't always possible between a field spook and those in the "normal" world. However, the friendships that do survive can become closer than most of those that regular civilians enjoy. That's because over time, understandings are reached, and the weight of the trust that is shared is, itself, a profound bond.

Bottom Line: The field spook personality at home can be endlessly varied. Some covert spooks will need to tell their spouses about their work, but they will likely keep their friends and family outside the IC in the dark. Some field spooks will *never* discuss their work with their spouses, children, or friends.

THE FIELD SPOOK MISSION PERSONALITY

Regardless of what field spooks are like when at home, they must be expert at subverting their civilian personalities to focus on a mission. All politics, ball teams, family, and anything else from the home life must be checked at the door as their world focuses down to the pinpoint of the mission.

When shifting into the mission personality, operatives are still themselves, but they might need to adapt to different behavior requirements depending on the mission and location. For example, they might need to adopt a different language, physical appearance, clothing, hand gestures, eating habits, accent, or slang in order to blend in and accomplish their goals. This mental shift of compartmentalizing the home personality begins before they reach the first briefing, and it doesn't start to shift back until they are on the plane home.

During a mission, a day in the life of a spook depends completely on that mission. The mission defines the spook's life, from the way they dress and eat to the way they speak and think. Every legend or cover is unique. Every mission is unique. There is only one commonality to every spook and every mission—there are no days off. There aren't even any minutes off. They have to be on their game all the time, even while asleep. A spook takes on their legend 100 percent. If they don't, there is extreme danger of giving themselves away.

In the field, a spook must be alert without being paranoid. At the same time, they must not appear to be anxious or *overly* alert. One trick they might use to achieve this is to take on particular personality traits that might not be their own. They might act like they love gourmet Italian food, they might take an interest in fine whiskies, or they might be an avid soccer fan. What this does is give the spook something other than the mission to discuss or share with the target group. The only caveat is that the character trait must be consistent with the mission, meaning it must be something that the target group can understand and accept.

For example, say a spook is going undercover as an arms runner. Arms runners tend to be filthy, greedy characters. The spook would choose a trait consistent with filthy, greedy characters, such as being a womanizer. They would connect with the arms runners by talking about women in crude and disgusting ways.

In another example, if the spook is posing as a Russian bartender near a military base, they have to appear to be a viable bartender. A Russian bartender would be constantly worried about getting paid and paying their bills, so the spook might take on more of a concern for money.

Whatever the trait is, though, the spook is committed to it for the duration of the mission. If they are pretending to be an avid soccer fan while undercover in Nigeria, it wouldn't do for them to suddenly not care who wins the World Cup.

In selecting this trait, the spook must avoid certain characteristics. They must never appear to be anxious or impatient. Such traits would be a red flag to the target group. And clearly, they can't become heroin addicts or heavy drinkers as their point of connection to the target group. It must be a trait consistent with the mission that will not incapacitate the spook or cause concern within the target group.

Whatever the mission personality is, it must be dominant and consistent throughout the mission until the plane ride home.

Bottom Line: The home personality is left at home, and every day in the field, a spook must be fully alert to the mission and to their own legend.

3

THE SPOOK CHARACTER

UNLIKE HOLLYWOOD, IN REAL LIFE SPOOKS *MUST* BE OF STRONG moral character.

ADDICTION ISSUES

While spooks can be animal lovers, gardeners, or World of Warcraft players, what spooks *can't* be, at least going in, are drunks, junkies, or gambling addicts. Addiction issues are an absolute no-go in the IC hiring process, in spite of any Hollywood and New York publishing myths to the contrary. The *only* exception to this is that a person can be eligible for regular employment if they have been clean and sober for an unspecified period of time. It's going to be a judgment call in every case, and it will depend upon the access that person would have to sensitive material. If an employee develops an addiction during the course of their career, such as an addiction to pain killers due to an injury, their retention will be evaluated on a case-by-case basis.

While a heroin, cocaine, or meth addiction is *always* a no-go for regular employees, there is a little bit more leeway with CIA contractors who have lesser-addiction issues. This leeway depends upon the type of contract and the amount and sensitivity of any information the contractor might access. That's because some contracts don't require much information exchange for the contractors to complete the task. For example, a contract for shipping sealed crates would be relatively low risk, as little sensitive information would be exchanged.

The CIA will still keep track of the contractor and how the contractor acts out. If the contractor acts out in their addiction at an inappropriate time, they get fired. If the contractor only indulges in their addiction on free time, the CIA will not fire them, but it will also never transfer them over to a regular employee job with reams of sensitive information going across their desk. That individual would be isolated from certain intelligence positions.

The CIA will be stricter with contractors that have addiction issues than it will be with subcontractors that have addiction issues. If a subcontractor's addiction issues do not interfere with their work performance and they are not exposed to any classified information, the agency might turn a blind eye to those addiction issues to varying degrees.

Intelligence organizations other than the CIA have various rules regarding addiction issues, and each agency must use its own judgment as to what it will tolerate from its employees, contractors, and subcontractors. These rules may seem simple on paper, but their application is complex. The behavior tolerated will depend upon how much exposure the person will have to classified information and how much contact they will have with an enemy, either inside or outside of the United States. The individual's skills and job performance are also taken into consideration. As a general rule, the higher the access a person has, the more concern the organization will have about any kind of substance abuse or addiction issues. Impeccable character is key.

Bottom Line: Addiction issues are a no-go during the hiring process for regular employment in the CIA and the Intelligence Community in general. There is some latitude for conditions that develop after hiring, and retention depends on the strength of the individual's performance. Contractors and subcontractors with issues that are not too severe are evaluated on a case-by-case basis.

Writing Tip: Many audiences love and relate to substance-abuse issues. While such issues are usually unrealistic with regular CIA employees, your characters that are contractors or subcontractors could provide worlds of conflict and issues that will make them highly relatable to readers.

CRIMINAL HISTORY

Another no-go for employment with the CIA and other intelligence organizations is a criminal history that displays a lack of ethical boundaries, such as rape, child abuse, or armed robbery. However, a criminal past is not an automatic deal breaker for the CIA. In fact, the CIA appreciates and utilizes clever criminal tendencies that do not cross base ethical boundaries. A small run-in with the law might be overlooked if it was far enough in the past. For example, one shoplifting arrest as a teenager won't bar a person from being hired. On the other hand, seven or eight shoplifting arrests would indicate a character issue. Such things are evaluated on a case-by-case basis.

> **Bottom Line:** Kids being kids is no big deal. Kids or adults who cross basic ethical boundaries is a deal breaker.

SHAME

Another deal breaker can be how a person feels about their own behavior and past, whether it is criminal or not. Spooks must be shameless, as in, they can't be hiding anything that an individual or a foreign entity could blackmail them about. People who carry shame are particularly vulnerable to being manipulated. It doesn't matter if they are hiding the fact that they shoplifted a piece of gum from Mr. Munson's store back when they were eleven, or if they had an ongoing affair with Mr. Munson, who was also their brother. What matters is how they feel about it. If they carry enough shame about whatever it is to be blackmailed, they are susceptible to control by foreign agents. As a result, spooks tend to be a rather more conservative lot than most people would suspect.

> **Bottom Line:** Intelligence operatives must be impervious to blackmail.

CHARACTER TRAITS ALL SPOOKS SHARE

While spooks can have a wide variety of personalities, religions, political opinions, and backgrounds, American spooks all have some character traits in common.

1. Highly Developed Mental Discipline

Spooks must be able to compartmentalize information, as well as their experiences. They must mentally wall off the work life from the personal life, and vice versa. Otherwise, they would talk out of turn, get burned out, or worse, if a field operative, they would get dead.

2. Love of Travel and Experiencing Foreign Cultures

One reason spooks are drawn to the work is an abiding interest in people, cultures, and experiencing their world.

3, Recognition That Diverse People Actually Are Diverse

Anyone can talk about diversity, and frequently they do so in the academic context of explaining away crucial differences as being irrelevant. Spooks, on the other hand, must live those differences, and they know that recognizing and understanding the contrasting values, personalities, and customs of other cultures is paramount to both their survival and the success of their missions. They must work within that kaleidoscopic framework on behalf of American interests.

4. Superior Intelligence

Spooks really do have to be smart.

We know what you're thinking ... But there's this spook on [fill in the network] that says really stupid things. Yes. We often laugh at them and wonder what they're up to. With spooks, as with everyone, intelligence is a tool that is dependent on the user, and it can always be limited or even nullified by character and hubris. We refer back to the Greatest Mistake mentioned in the intro.

5. They Are Wholly Committed

Spooks are not wishy-washy people, whether they spend their career at an analyst's desk at Headquarters or in Third World countries hunting down our enemies. They commit their time, their relationships, and even their lives in service to our nation. They are people who sacrifice on many levels—some even sacrificing their lives—and sacrifice is the heart of commitment. The clandestine services take a piece from everyone who serves.

6. Good Sense of Humor

Even the field spooks like Holmes, whose spirit animal is Grumpy Cat, have a great sense of humor. Without it, they would go mad in short order.

7. Loyalty

Spooks are loyal to America and to the *ideals* of the US Constitution and US society. This is not a blind loyalty or a fanaticism, but rather a deep commitment that makes them willing to sacrifice their lifestyle and potentially their lives in service to our country.

8. Socially Accepting

Religion, race, ethnicity, first language, and financial background are irrelevant to spooks as compared to skill and loyalties. In fact, such differences are highly valued and useful as long as the individuals are first and foremost loyal to America and to American constitutional ideals. The field is a meritocracy, and what matters most is who can get the job done and come home alive.

9. Covert Action Spooks Can Get Wild During Recess

Field spooks, specifically, have a "certain skill set" that lends them to being a bit wilder than the average bear when letting off steam. We aren't providing examples in order to protect the guilty.

Writing Tip: When your field spook characters are blowing off steam, let your imagination out to play. To be realistic, though, just make certain anyone on the wrong end of a prank or an international incident is completely deserving.

---

10. Counter-Intelligence ("CI") Spooks Are Sober and Intensely Patient

CI spooks are looking for that one irregularity—that one glowing clue. Or to sink to a cliché because it is so apt, the needle in the haystack, and they have to sift through tons of hay. CI spooks keep track of mountains of information and are highly skilled at catching that one anomaly or inconsistency in evaluating a foreign agent or in locating a mole within their organization. That requires the soul of patience and attention to detail.

The overriding trait common to spooks, particularly to field spooks, is a farsighted optimism. It is a belief that what they are doing is helping to make their country safer for those back at home. It is the conviction that when they risk their lives, it is for a better tomorrow.

"If I didn't believe I was helping create a better world, I would never jump out of the plane." ~ Jay Holmes

---

4

SPOOK RECRUITMENT

DURING WORLD WAR II, INTELLIGENCE ORGANIZATIONS SNATCHED up exceptionally bright, capable students at their time of graduation. As in, *snatched up*. One scientist we know literally came home to find half of his belongings loaded up in a moving van upon his graduation from MIT. He was met by government officials at his house and swiftly relocated to Los Alamos to work on the Manhattan Project. Such strong-arm recruitment methods were specific to that time period, when the future of America was in great peril. Today, intelligence organizations have less forceful methods of recruiting, such as web sites.

CIA WEB SITE

One way a spook can be recruited is to simply apply on the web site. The CIA site provides extensive explanations about the experience and qualities they're seeking in applicants, as well as job descriptions and application forms. If an applicant passes the first round, they then take a battery of tests online. The third round could include a phone interview, which could then progress to background checks and face-to-face interviews in DC. The process can take well over a year to complete.

COLLEGE CAMPUSES

It is also now common to see the CIA, NSA, FBI, etc., recruiting on college campuses from booths on Career Day. It's been known for some of these agencies to sit in on interviews students have with other agencies in order to spot or even poach potential talent. In that eventuality, the CIA recruiter would provide the interviewee with a business card and invite them to call.

The IC also has Intelligence Community Centers at twenty-one universities across the nation. At these universities, students can apply to be IC Scholars. Also, the University of New Mexico became the first CIA Signature School in November of 2016. Students at that university can apply to the National Security Scholars Program and earn a National Security and Strategic Analysis Certification. The IC has targeted these universities because of their high rates of student diversity. As we discuss later in this book, diversity has always been a positive in the Intelligence Community, particularly for field spooks.

Many agencies even have college internships available, and some of them are well paid, including benefits and potential employment contracts for students with talent, ambition, and the confidence to apply. Desirable majors include everything from geography and languages to engineering and economics. During the internship, the college student is given training in more than one area and exposure to the Intelligence Community culture. However, the student would not be sent on clandestine missions unless they had previous military experience, and likely not even then.

Writing Tip: Piper's son reports, to his amusement, that the NSA recruiters at his campus are little old ladies. We take this as an indication that writers have a great deal of latitude with the age and experience of various IC Career Day recruiters they might want to include in their books.

How the CIA Does *Not* Recruit from Campuses

There is one way the CIA definitely does *not* recruit from campuses. Some folks may recall that a couple of years ago, a major New York publisher released an "autobiography" of a "covert operative" who claimed to be so brilliant and capable that the CIA pulled him out of college and gave him a mission before he had even completed his training. Yeah, no. Doesn't happen. The guy is alleged far and wide to be a total fraud, but his book is still on the market. You'll know it when you see it. We don't recommend it.

> *"Don't believe everything you read."* ~ Every Reasoning Person Since Hieroglyphs Were Invented

A slightly different scenario *has* been known to occur at college campuses on rare occasions, though. It is possible for someone with previous military training to be recruited by the CIA and to serve in clandestine operations while they are attending college. If the spook could talk about it, it would make for an interesting "What I Did Last Summer" paper in English 101.

OTHER ROADS TO IC EMPLOYMENT

As in any enterprise, there is no formal structure for the informal structure. However, if someone has an excellent character and specific skills, the winding path could lead to the IC door.

For example, at times military personnel catch the attention of the CIA. On those rare occasions, the CIA will approach them at the end of their enlistment or contract time to discuss possible employment with them.

Word-of-mouth recommendations can also lead to employment. For example, if a clandestine operator is putting together a team and knows someone with a particular set of skills, that operator may take steps to bring the person into the fold.

Former employees are also a recruitment pool. If a mission involves a talent or ability that a former spook is known for, the CIA might approach that former employee and attempt to persuade them to work for them again, either as a returned employee or as a contractor.

The NSA in particular keeps its able ear to the ground to locate hackers who are suitable for employment, and that agency tries to snap them all up. However, the NSA doesn't get them all. The CIA recruits its own hackers as well.

Bottom Line: The CIA is an open-minded and versatile organization, where at times the personnel manual gets tossed out the window.

TWO ABSOLUTE NO-NOS

That being said, there are two ways the CIA never recruits under any circumstances.

First, it never blackmails anyone to work for them as an employee . . . We know. *The Man from U.N.C.L.E.* was a hoot of a movie. We enjoyed it, too, but no . . . The Company never has to do that. It already has more applicants than positions. Also, someone being blackmailed can't be trusted.

Second, the IC never approaches minors to recruit them. Sorry to disappoint, but Cody Banks isn't real. The Intelligence Community is not allowed to discuss specific job opportunities with anyone under the age of eighteen.

We know what some of you writers are thinking . . . But what if I'm writing for Young Adults? Doesn't the CIA approach high schoolers?

In a word, no. The CIA does not approach individual high school students to recruit them. Not ever. The closest it gets to that is advertising its college internship program mentioned above.

Writing Tip: Young Adult writers have two options. The first is obvious. It's fiction, so you can make something up. There is a more realistic route, though. The character can enlist in the military at seventeen and, through test scores and demonstrated abilities, be selected for a top-secret military intelligence program. With intense training, they could be in the field by the age of nineteen.

Side Note: If any of you readers decide your current career aspirations need a backup plan and apply to the CIA, don't tell anyone. It could limit your opportunities in the agency.

5
SPOOK TRAINING, A.K.A. TRADECRAFT

TRADECRAFT FOR THE FIELD VARIES FOR EVERY SPOOK AND DEPENDS largely on what the individual brings to the party. For example, if their native language is Spanish, they won't need Spanish language classes. Also, many people who work in clandestine operations and covert action come to the CIA from a military background. They've already received various types and qualities of training before they continue into civilian service, and that will determine what type of training is required to prepare them for their spook life.

But everyone, regardless of the position they will fill with the CIA, still requires some training in the CIA culture. That training emphasizes standard operating procedures, securing operations and information, and the standards they're expected to uphold as members of the CIA or any other intelligence organization.

Training also depends on the mission at hand. If the spook needs combat training or dive training, they will get it. If they need training in foreign languages, they will get it. If they need training in lock picking and bugging, they will get it. And if they need training in shooting, they will get it. However, mission efficiency dictates that the spook who is already most suited for the mission will most likely be the spook to be tasked with the mission.

Some covert operations can be highly kinetic and involve numerous combat situations. However, the shooting, blowing up, and killing aspects are fairly minimal to spook work and far less common than people assume from what they've learned in books and movies. More often, a successful mission relies on deception and stealth. Because of this wide variety of missions, a wide variety of skills and people are necessary, and the perfect spook for one operation might be wholly unqualified for the next.

Tradecraft for a deep-cover operative is shaped around the operative's legend, or cover story. If their job will be working in a café a half block from a Chinese military headquarters, they'll probably never be expected to go into that headquarters or to go out and meet with agents. Their job would be to simply observe. Someone in that position may have some training in placing and retrieving bugs, but they wouldn't need to know lock picking, shooting, or how to blow a door. Let's face the facts. If they're half a block from a Chinese military headquarters and they need to know how to shoot, it won't change a thing. They're screwed. Working in a foreign café while watching a building would be a completely inglorious mission, and it wouldn't make a good movie, but it would be an important mission, nonetheless. Many field missions are just so.

Bottom Line: Training is tailored to the spook and to the mission.

6
THE ROLE OF WOMEN IN ESPIONAGE

THE ROLE OF WOMEN IN ESPIONAGE MISSIONS IS DETERMINED ON A case-by-case basis. There are times when it's preferred to have a female operative on a task. For example, if the goal is to place someone near another country's First Lady or other powerful people, a female can gain entry where a male could not.

One famous example of this sort of placement is Aline, Dowager Countess of Romanones. Aline Griffith was a model for Hattie Carnegie in New York during WWII when she was cajoled into attending a small dinner party, where she met John Derby, an official in the young Office of Strategic Services ("OSS"). When talk turned to the war, Aline, unaware of John Derby's profession, stated that she wanted to serve overseas, as her brothers were doing. Derby made that happen by drafting her into the OSS.

At the age of twenty, Aline was sent to Spain as a cipher clerk, working under diplomatic cover for the American Oil Mission in Madrid. Her additional mission was to gain admittance into upper-crust Spanish social circles for the purpose of uncovering Himmler's top spy in Madrid. Her beauty and education were a ticket into high society. She soon befriended the daughters of the

Spanish nobility and became a regular at their soirées and house parties. Her account of her experiences during this exciting time in history can be found in her autobiography, *The Spy Wore Red*.

Aline continued to work for the OSS in Europe after the war until she resigned in 1947 to marry the Count of Quintanilla. She told him shortly before their wedding that she was a spook on behalf of America, but he thought she was joking. According to her second book, *The Spy Went Dancing*, when he finally realized she was serious, he was not amused. They worked it out.

The CIA has been a historical front-runner in nondiscrimination, long recognizing the unique contributions of minorities, women, foreign-born patriots, and the disabled. This is particularly true in the field, where women fill every position from courier to chief of station. And at the time of publication of this book, the first female director of the CIA, Gina Haspel, had just been sworn in.

VIRGINIA HALL

One WWII operator, Virginia Hall, is an example of just what women are charged with in the field. Correction, "disabled" women.

Virginia was a young consular service clerk at the consulate office in Izmir, Turkey, when she accidentally shot her leg off in a hunting accident. She was fitted with a wooden leg she named "Cuthbert." Then she was reassigned to Venice, Italy. She asked permission to take the US Foreign Service Exam but was told that she could not because of her injury. After attending graduate school at American University, Virginia went to work for the British Special Operations Executive ("SOE").

In 1941, Virginia became the first British SOE agent to infiltrate Vichy, France. She rescued hundreds of downed Allied aviators, arranged their safe return to England, organized a network of safe houses, and coordinated numerous airdrops of weapons and supplies to the French Resistance. The Gestapo branded "The Limping Lady" as the most dangerous spy in all of France and made her capture a priority. In November of 1942, Virginia escaped the Gestapo by crossing the Pyrenees. Alone. In the snow. Still with one leg. Bad. Ass. In 1943, England's King George VI presented Virginia Hall with an honorary membership in the Order of the British Empire for her courage and successes.

Virginia wasn't finished. She went to work for the American OSS, the precursor to the CIA, and slipped back into Nazi-occupied France to continue her work with the French Resistance and the Allied forces. In September of 1945, on behalf of a grateful nation, OSS General William "Wild Bill" Donovan presented Virginia Hall with a Distinguished Service Cross. It was the highest honor received by any female civilian during WWII.

Virginia Hall Receiving Distinguished Service Cross from OSS
General William "Wild Bill" Donovan
Image Public Domain

But Virginia still wasn't finished. She went to work undercover in Italy operating against Soviet efforts to cultivate Italian communist groups. Afterward, she worked with a CIA front group, the National Committee for a Free Europe, which was associated with Radio Free Europe.

In 1950, Virginia married OSS Agent Paul Goillot, and the following year both she and her husband joined the newly established CIA. She became an expert on resistance groups in Soviet-occupied Europe and remained in the shadows, working on a variety of projects, until her retirement in 1966.

Virginia Hall Goillot passed away of natural causes at Shady Grove Adventist Hospital in Rockville, Maryland, on July 8, 1982. To this day, her remarkable history of selfless service in the cause of freedom remains a shining example for the intrepid few who might dare to follow in her footsteps. For more about Virginia Hall, see *Key Figures in Espionage: The Good, the Bad, and the Booty*.

Virginia is only one example of outstanding women operatives. According to Holmes and based on his forty-plus years of personal experience, if he were scoring by gender, he would give women overall slightly higher marks for intelligence work for several reasons.

First, as a general rule with some definite exceptions, women are outstanding at managing information—keeping it secure, interpreting it, massaging it, categorizing it, etc.

Second, women are excellent at knowing when to cross-reference to pertinent information. For many of the best female intelligence professionals, there's no such thing as a closed file, and if there is a piece of missing or suspicious information, they'll remember it and reference back to it ten or twenty years later, even without turning on a computer. When they do turn the computer on, they already know what they're looking for. (Piper would point out that many husbands would say they have also experienced this phenomenon with their wives.)

Third, women are outstanding at respecting compartmentalization and, overall, women are less likely to violate compartmentalization of information than some of the male employees. In other words, women are actually a bit better than men at keeping their mouths shut.

And fourth, women are excellent at spotting inconsistencies in a target. It's no accident that it was two women who ferreted out Aldrich Ames, a CIA employee spying for the Russians. We tell more about that dirtbag in our chapter on the CIA a bit later in the book.

Don't get us wrong. *Many* male operatives are *outstanding* at managing information. However, in Holmes's experience, a higher percentage of women operatives excel at these information-management skills.

SPECIAL OPERATIONS

That being said, men definitely have a niche where they hands-down dominate, and that is the area of military special operations. Women are certainly not excluded from this "heavy lifting," but it would be extremely unusual for a female to go along with the male special operators on a clandestine mission in the jungles or mountains. The vast majority of women are not as strong as the average man. When one considers that special operators are not average men, but the strongest of men, this lack of physical potential almost precludes women from completing much of the training necessary for special operations.

Reality isn't politically correct. Physical attributes are not politically correct. The most physically demanding work of special operators remains the *nearly* exclusive territory of men. While there may be a rare exception, this female will definitely have the emphasis on "rare."

WOMEN ASSASSINS

Genuine assassinations are rare, and finding an assassin is easier than getting a target approved. That's because for a US spook, an assassination requires approval directly from the president, and it is no small request. In fact, according to public policy history, President Ronald Reagan banned CIA executions with Executive Order 12333. Public policy lightened up on such matters after 9/11.

Should an assassination request be granted, either a man or a woman could do the job. It would depend completely on what works best for the individual operation. Note that an assassination is very different from killing someone in the field during a kinetic incident. That can happen to people of any gender on any given bad day.

Bottom Line: If a woman is the best person for the mission, a woman will be selected. Any limitations on women in the field are purely due to the physical reality of actual strength capabilities.

Writing Tip: Be generous with your female spooks' abilities and experiences. Women have always been essential to the IC, and it has long been populated with sharp, capable ladies at every level.

7
FIFTY SHADES OF "COVERT"

THE INTELLIGENCE COMMUNITY IS VAST AND VARIED, FROM janitors to analysts to deep-cover operatives. While everyone must be discreet to varying degrees, few are *truly* covert, and exactly how covert and how long they are covert varies with the type of work they do. We will focus primarily on CIA officers and operatives, as they are the most written about in spy fiction.

EMPLOYEES, STAFF, AND HEADQUARTERS

Every day, CIA employees park in the parking lot of CIA headquarters in Virginia. They walk in through the front door of the building, badge in with the blue badges they carry in their purses or pockets, and they are listed in the in-house directory. They may be serving in the Company as analysts, janitors, administrators, human resources officers, interns, or in any number of other positions.

Regardless of their function inside that headquarters building, their work is not a discussion around the holiday table with gathered family. Depending on the nature of their positions, they might not even tell their family where they work, and they would not tell any friends outside their "need to know" zone. They will likely even have a cover story to tell family members, friends, and neighbors. The more critical and important their work, the more mundane their story will be. But does that make them genuinely "covert"? Not necessarily. "Covert" is not as well-defined as it might seem to be.

It can be argued that no one who drives through the front gate, parks in the parking lot at CIA Headquarters, carries a blue badge *on their person*, walks through the front door of Headquarters, and/or is listed in the in-house directory is truly currently "covert." Think about it. All a determined enemy would have to do to blow the employee's cover is follow them to work, watch the front gate, search their pockets, or read the directory.

That being said, those who operate as genuinely covert CIA operatives abroad would still typically park in the parking lot and badge in through the front door when they go to Headquarters. The most *certain* definition of "not covert" that CIA employees can likely agree on is that if an employee is listed in the in-house directory, they are not covert, no matter what they tell their friends, families, politicians, or publishers.

Sometimes spooks start out badging in daily through the front door of Headquarters and then go undercover in the field. Sometimes those in the field "come in from the Cold" and work at Headquarters. In other words, not everyone who works covertly is locked into anonymity for the rest of their lives, and a spook who starts out "not particularly covert" is not necessarily prevented from living a cover story at some point in their career.

It also might happen that someone who has been *truly* covert will reach a point in their career when it is safe for themselves and others if they come out of the Intelligence Community closet. However, once they do, the organization they worked for no longer has a duty to maintain their anonymity. In other words, a spook cannot "out" themself, even in private meetings with publishers to pitch their career story, and then cry foul because the government no longer invests in their cover.

We know what you're thinking. . . . But wait! I heard about an analyst who worked at Headquarters that got "outed" and went on to make a fortune with a book and a movie.

Yeah. We know about that one, too. . . . It is not unheard of for a badge-in-daily-through-the-front-door employee or former employee who was listed in the in-house directory to cash in on the public's misperception that they were in deep cover for the purposes of publication. In fact, the news industry and publishing houses everywhere love that kind of "covert" operative because they can plaster the person's face and yard-long résumé about their covertness across billboards to make a mint off of books, media articles, and even political scandals.

We would note that it is possible to imagine that some intelligence organizations within the IC would have a use for personnel who are only known to a handful of people within that organization. With such a spook, the organization would hold their badge for them, and they might rarely or never go to Headquarters. If they did have an imperative reason to go to Headquarters, they would enter the building by some other means than with a blue badge at the front door. If at some point they ever did choose to lead a "front door life," their badges would be given to them for their use.

While employees who walk in through the front door of CIA Headquarters may not all be covert, the actual headquarters building, on the other hand, is another story. While the front-door employees and staff may be discreet, the building itself is under a blanket of secrecy. When an employee or contractor walks through that door, absolutely everything inside is classified. That means no one is legally allowed to discuss anything they find inside that building, right down to the color of paint on the walls or the lunch menu in the cafeteria, unless they are given specific permission to do so. This holds true for all CIA facilities.

> **Bottom Line:** The CIA building itself is more covert than some of the spooks who walk in and out of its front door to work, but those spooks still aren't going to chat about their jobs over coffee or on social media without permission to do so.

> **Writing Tip:** If someone is listed in the organization's in-house directory, they are not covert. The vast majority of your characters, even those who are covert while abroad, will at some point carry organizational badges on their persons and walk in through the front door of Headquarters. Characters who are deeply covert, even within the IC, must have an imperative reason for going to Headquarters, and when they do, they won't badge in through the front. You can feel free to bust out your imagination when getting those operatives into the building.

DIPLOMATIC COVER

The State Department maintains embassies and consulates around the world. Generally, the CIA enjoys picking on the State Department—they're the suits. In its turn, the State Department views the CIA as its reckless neighbors. Some CIA officers and operatives joke that the State Department facilities only exist for the purpose of giving spooks cover. That's because they actually do—give spooks cover, that is. It is a known practice for countries to insert their intelligence operatives into foreign countries under diplomatic cover. In other words, countries mix in their spooks with their diplomats. The United States is no different on that score.

At US installations, CIA officers and operatives share embassy or consulate space with military attachés and actual diplomats. This allows the intelligence personnel to blend into the country under the appearance of being diplomats. It provides the spooks with "diplomatic cover" and gives them diplomatic immunity if ever arrested.

Spooks under diplomatic cover, and sometimes their spouses, can expect to be under surveillance twenty-four hours a day. Other than that fact, they can lead relatively normal lives, as compared to their professional cousins who are in a country without diplomatic cover. The spooks under diplomatic cover can go have lunch in the embassy, enjoy an affair with their secretary, and tell people their real names and locations.

Though their operations are separate from the State Department, spooks living under diplomatic cover intentionally socialize with the State Department diplomats. This provides the spooks with two main benefits. First, in most countries these visible interactions help keep the spooks from being made by the local spies. And second, the State Department employees give the spooks an added network they would not otherwise have.

One of the favorite pastimes of spooks living under diplomatic cover is a game called Spot the Spook. Spot the Spook is all about observing the personnel of other countries' embassies and identifying the spies among them. Holmes would point out that while this may be both entertaining and useful for those with diplomatic cover, it can also be dangerous, particularly for spooks without diplomatic cover, as the spooks being spotted might also be spotting back.

> *"The quickest way to spot a spook is to spot who's spotting you back, and then you're screwed."* ~ Jay Holmes

The US State Department diplomats in our overseas installations don't just view CIA personnel as their reckless neighbors, they actually refer to the intelligence personnel in their buildings as "the neighbors." Interestingly, the UK embassy diplomats also refer to their MI6 cousins in their buildings as "the neighbors," and even Russian diplomats refer to the Russian spies who share their buildings the same way. The term "the neighbors" seems to reflect a fairly universal relationship between diplomats and their coordinate intelligence communities.

Intelligence officers and operatives under diplomatic cover handle foreign agents and collect intelligence any way they can without generating evidence that they are not actually diplomats. How they achieve these goals can vary from country to country. In an allied country, such as the UK or Canada, our spooks are most likely to simply ask the UK or Canadian liaison to the government for whatever information it is they need. Achieving goals in hostile countries such as Russia, China, or Iran, however, is a far more intricate and dangerous proposition. For simplicity's sake, we will explain in terms of Russia, but the explanation also applies to China and, to varying degrees, to other hostile nations.

In a hostile country such as Russia, an operative's diplomatic cover is blown the minute they get off the plane. Russians are very good at distinguishing diplomats from intelligence personnel. The trick is for the intelligence personnel to never give Russia proof.

For example, because of the high need for vigilance in protecting our foreign agents in Russia, our spooks almost never go to a dead drop, which is a location where tangible items are transferred. They also almost never meet with a foreign agent directly. Instead, they use "cutouts."

Cutouts are people who stand between the foreign agent and the operative. When a foreign agent wants to send information or anything else to the operative, that agent will pass the information to a cutout. The cutout will then pass it on to the operative or another cutout in the chain. There could be any number of cutouts, though more than three would be rare. Also, the same cutouts would never be used for two exchanges with the same foreign agent in a row. An operative can never afford to forget that every foreign agent and every cutout could be a double agent, and that any and every person in the chain could be potentially caught and tortured into revealing secrets.

In order to meet with a cutout or an agent, an operative must "go clean," or, in other words, they must not be under surveillance. This is exceptionally difficult in hostile countries, so going to a meet is a group effort.

Say, for example, seven operatives* are stationed in the US Embassy in Moscow. If one of them needs to meet with a cutout or an agent, the other six go out as well and draw heat. The other six will do everything they can from wearing transmitters to frequenting places where Russians would expect American spooks to go. Sometimes the spooks drawing heat will make sure they don't quite lose their Russian tail. Sometimes they will work hard to shake the tail, as if they really mean business. The point is to tie up Russian spies and get as many Russian eyes as possible away from the seventh spook—the one that is actually meeting with a cutout or a foreign agent.

This elaborate dance is necessary because the most critical piece of spycraft for running foreign agents is conducting any contact with those agents or cutouts, whether face-to-face or collecting from a dead drop. It's at that point of contact that spooks are most commonly caught by the enemy. That is true for spies with other governments as well as for our own spooks.

Back to our seventh spook in Russia and the meet. While six spooks are keeping as many Russian spies busy as possible, the seventh spook goes out and does anything they have to do to lose their watchers. They run through restaurants, climb out windows, change their clothing at prearranged sites, etc. It is imperative that they lose their tail before they meet up with a cutout or an agent. The spook and their foreign agent must not get caught.

"Even one mistake is two mistakes too many." ~ Jay Holmes

If the operative *is* caught passing information with a cutout or an agent, two things will happen. First, the spook will be on the next plane home. If in Russia, it could take twenty-four hours or so. That's because the Russians like to harass people for a while before booting them out. Second, and more serious, the cutout or agent will be imprisoned, tortured for information, and executed in a horrific manner. For example, the common way that the Soviets executed our foreign agents during the Cold War was to shoot them or to feed them into a crematorium, feet first, one inch at a time.

We know what you're thinking . . . But that was the Soviet Union. Glad they're gone.

No. Think of Russia as the Reorganized Union of Soviet Socialists In Asia, led by a man who is KGB to the core—Vladimir Putin. Think of Putin as Stalin 2.0. Putin is a bit different from his predecessors in how he handles those who spy against Russia. When caught, the little fish just disappear. A bigger fish is put on trial for their crimes, but the agent isn't just tried for spying against Russia. Putin goes to the trouble of framing the traitor with a major scandal.

Putin doesn't just want big-name agents and cutouts to go down for spying for the United States or the West because too many people in Russia today are sympathetic to the West. Instead, Putin routinely frames those agents for heinous crimes such as pedophilia, rape, corruption, or embezzlement, painting them as social deviants. Sometimes Putin's people will even commit those crimes in order to frame the agent. Putin doesn't want to just shoot the transgressors. Putin wants the public to routinely associate spying for the West with perversion and depravity.

Bottom line: Foreign agents and cutouts in hostile countries risk everything to meet with our operatives. Their lives literally depend on the integrity of our administration, the skill of our Intelligence Community, and the strength of our national security procedures.

Writing Tip: Feel free to run wild with the action and drama when your spook characters are shaking their watchers. Characters can hide in laundry trucks, run across roofs of buildings, swap out wigs, switch out cars, or do anything else that is necessary to lose their tails.

---

*We can neither confirm nor deny whether seven operatives are stationed at the US Embassy in Moscow. Truth is, we have no flaming idea how many are there, nor do we have any business knowing that. Seven is an arbitrary number.

SPECIAL OPERATIONS

> *"We sleep soundly in our beds because rough men stand ready in the night to visit violence upon those who would do us harm."* ~ George Orwell or Winston Churchill—No one seems to be quite sure who said it first.

"Special operations" are unconventional military operations involving unconventional methods and resources that are carried out by dedicated military special operations forces units.

We've all heard of some special operations branches—SEALs, Marine Raiders, and Delta Force. The existence of these groups and the operators in them is not, in and of itself, covert. Those who serve in these groups might not advertise the fact, or they might put it in their Facebook and Twitter bios. They might even write books about their experiences. However, while the organizations and their members are not necessarily covert, their missions definitely are. Everything about a mission is classified until the mission command says differently.

We've all see the "untold stories" or the "real account" that at least allegedly contains the "uncensored" true stories of missions. They supposedly reveal the truth the government didn't want anyone to hear. Guaranteed the Pentagon and White House knew about them before they were released, and they were allowed to exist because either the administration did not deem them to be compromising, or because something in them was politically advantageous to the administration.

That doesn't mean that the author won't be taken to task at a later date, at least to keep up appearances. Even if classified information is broadcast to the world by a vice president or other politicians, the operatives on the mission are not legally allowed to talk about it until they are given permission by their command to do so.

Some readers may recall the book *No Easy Day*, written by former US Navy SEAL Matt Bissonnette, who was part of the bin Laden mission. Bissonnette claimed that nothing he said in the book wasn't already out in the public through other avenues. Also, no one in the Pentagon stopped the presses or had the book pulled after its release. Nevertheless, the Pentagon threatened the former SEAL with prison, and Bissonnette had to forfeit $6.8 million in book royalties and speaking fees.

Special Operations and Social Media

We know what you're thinking . . . But what about when the information is all over social media? Is it still covert?

Social media presents particular challenges to the clandestine community.

"You're only covert until the first shot is fired." ~ Jay Holmes and Every Other Spook Since Firearms Were Invented

---

As soon as that first shot is fired, others can become aware of the operators' presence. In the past, the concerns were that the enemy's reinforcements would appear, people would call the police, or bystanders would come out to see what was happening and get caught in the cross fire. While those are all still concerns, operatives now have the added danger of social media. People on Twitter, Instagram, Facebook, etc., could report the operation in real time.

"A helicopter just landed on the compound next door. At least a dozen guys getting out with rifles. One has a dog. #ASPCA #SaturdayNight"

"Holy crap! Check out this selfie I just got with the explosion. #Islamabad #selfie"

"Looks like they're hauling some guy out of there and shoving him onto the helicopter. #shouldbeamovie @JerryBruckheimer @OliverStone"

When missions hit social media, they are no longer covert, but they are still classified until mission command decides otherwise. Until the information is officially declassified, those involved in the mission are not allowed to discuss the mission.

> **Bottom Line:** SEALS, Raiders, Delta, and other publicly known groups of special operators are not themselves necessarily covert, but their missions are, and they are classified until their command says differently.

SPECIAL ACCESS PROGRAMS ("SAPs")

Unlike the SEALs, Raiders, Delta, and many other military commands, the very existence of Special Access Programs is as covert as covert can get. Those who know they exist are not allowed to speak of them. Those who are members of SAPs should never name their group. They will not tell their friends or family the organization they work with or specifically what they do, and they will not be authoring tell-all books. SAPs, their members, and their activities are *always* beyond Top Secret.

As an example, in a recent congressional investigation, the inspector general of the IC—the person who's supposed to keep everyone in the Intelligence Community in line—had to be "read in," or receive special permission, to even view evidence that referenced Special Access Programs. That is how top secret these programs are. We'd tell you more about SAPs, except we would and should be jailed if we did. So we won't be doing that.

Bottom Line: If you meet anyone who talks about SAPs, brags about being part of one, or e-mails about them outside of government-protected encrypted systems, please report them to the FBI. We'd like those people locked up.

Writing Tip: Special Access Programs provide great opportunities in fiction. There are far more letters in the alphabet than "C," "I," and "A." To be more creative and realistic, invent a Special Access Program for the characters. Name it anything at all, and have the characters do anything that is consistent with the spook ideals, character, and personality. No one will ever be able to prove you wrong. If you get a knock on your door some day from a team in Jos. A. Bank suits, you'll know you got it entirely too right.

DEEP-COVER OPERATIVES

A deep-cover operative is a spook that takes on a fictional name and background called a "legend" or "cover." They slip into a foreign country and blend in, frequently working with people in that country for a goal that serves their mutual interests. The mission could be any number of things from observing the comings and goings of terrorists or other foes, to providing support for other operatives, to hunting down and thwarting the agents of our enemies. The mission could last a few days, weeks, months, or even as long as two or three years, though three years would be a very long time for an American deep-cover operative.

Once a deep-cover operative returns home, the people they worked with are left behind in that foreign country. The opposition is also still there. Even if that opposition is defeated and their organization is dissolved, the individuals who were in those groups usually reorganize or join criminal enterprises. Those individuals have hard hearts and long memories. That is why many deep-cover operatives must do whatever is necessary to prevent anyone from connecting their real name and face with any kind of espionage.

For example, a deep-cover operative might take on the name Nazir and travel to Pakistan as Auntie Noorgul's nephew. While there, he might kill the head of a Taliban faction, steal important papers from the Russian Embassy, and/or spy on the Pakistani Intelligence Services. Then he might return home, go to college, get married, open a Pakistani bakery, and have a lovely daughter named after Auntie Noorgul.

If at any point in time it were to be revealed that Auntie Noorgul's nephew was working for the CIA or another intelligence agency, Auntie Noorgul would turn up dead. Mr. Auntie Noorgul would be dead. All of the little Noorguls and anyone associated with the "nephew" would become targets. Not only that, the operative and his or her family stateside would also possibly become targets. When a deep-cover operative goes into a foreign country and cultivates assets, it is a sacred trust to protect them. As a result, many deep-cover operatives have a lifelong obligation to maintain their anonymity.

> **Bottom Line:** When a true deep-cover operative is "outed," people can and do die. Even after they are outed, they won't be writing any *New York Times* bestsellers about their experiences or advising movie producers in the story of their life.

8

SPECIAL MESSAGE FOR PUBLISHERS

EVERY SO OFTEN, SOMEONE WILL LAND AN AGENT AND A PUBLISHER by wearing their "I'm A Spy" T-shirt and promising an exposé about the dirty secrets the Intelligence Community doesn't want anyone to know. They may claim to be a former CIA employee or contractor. They may call themselves by a fancy title such as "Certified Expert Master Counterterrorism Specialist." They may even claim to be a "former CIA hit man"—because *that's* a great idea, right? Because *no one* would want to hunt *them* down . . . Doh . . . Anyway, even the Big Five publishing houses periodically get sucked into this trap. And frankly, they deserve it if they are ready to publish national secrets in exchange for filthy lucre.

When a "spy" approaches a publisher with a "tell-all" book, one of four things is happening:

1. The person is lying.

"Thems that's talkin' ain't thems that's doin'." ~ Piper Bayard, in her best imitation of a wise Ozark granny

This is the most common occurrence, and some liars have succeeded in roping in agents and publishers, and even in perpetuating great societal myths about fictional historical events that are now accepted as "truth" and taught as such in history classes. Yes. We've actually seen that a couple of times since 9/11. And no. It's probably not the ones you think. But that is for another day. Our point is that a great number of people make a great deal of money when a liar pulls one off, either through intention or chance. The CIA gets a good laugh, and the world continues to turn.

In a more common example, a major publisher will release a book—such as the one referenced in the section on Spook Recruiting—with a great deal of fanfare and "no CIA vetting." The book will often confirm every radical "Evil CIA" conspiracy theory of the past forty years since audiences love such fodder. The publisher frequently finds out soon after the release that the "operative" was a flake and a con artist. Again, the CIA gets a good laugh, but the publisher loses out big time.

Publishers have a choice when someone comes in with the "tell-all" book. They can go for broke and publish it, taking the chance that they will succeed in perpetuating the latest, greatest societal myth rather than lose a great deal of money in an embarrassing scandal, or they can ask the CIA or any other agency if that person has ever worked with them.

The CIA does not volunteer information about its employees, and it is not allowed to say more about employees than the employees say about themselves. Many employees choose to be discreet about their employment, even if they are under no legal obligation to do so. The CIA honors that discretion. However, employees can't have it both ways. If an employee opens the door and blows their own cover, the CIA is under no obligation to lie on their behalf. In other words, if a publisher simply contacts the

CIA and tells them that Stevie Spysalot is in their office claiming to have been a top CIA employee, the CIA personnel office is allowed to confirm or deny Stevie's claim.

In fact, the CIA even has an Employment Verification Office for mortgage companies, creditors, and potential employers. Go to "www.CIA.gov," search on "Employment Verification Office," click on the link, and follow the instructions. Or go ahead and lose your ass with a fraud. It's your choice.

The FBI does less clandestine work and is generally more open about the identification of their employees. As a result, FBI agents are less likely to be cagey about their work situation, and the FBI is more forthcoming with information.

> **Bottom Line:** Regardless of which intelligence agency or organization with whom the "tell-all tattler" is claiming affiliation, a simple question can save a great deal of financial loss and embarrassment.

2. The person was in the Intelligence Community in some capacity, but they were never there long enough or deep enough to realize that no single employee knows enough to write a "tell-all" book.

Piper sees these folks on Twitter periodically, saying things like, "Everyone in Intelligence knows . . ." No. The Intelligence Community is like every other group of people. You get a dozen spooks in one place, and they might not all agree that the sun is shining at high noon on a cloudless day.

Often these "tell-all" types say they are former operatives or analysts. They sell themselves as knowing more than the director of the CIA, the president, and the ghost of Wild Bill Donovan put together. In truth, they may have been analysts or operatives, or they may have been on the cleaning crew or in the cafeteria. We have no idea how much access they had to important materials, and publishers have no way of knowing that, either. Again, we refer back to the Greatest Mistake. Everyone who is *good* at intelligence knows that they don't have enough information to write a tell-all anything.

3. The person really was a deep-cover operative, and they have become unhinged.

As explained above, when a true deep-cover operative is exposed, people often start to die. Only someone unhinged would want that. Still, publishers want to push ahead. It raises two questions for us:

1. Why would any publisher want to expose State secrets?
2. Why would any publisher want to expose our operatives and assets to torture and death?

If you are a publisher and you come across any actual important information, we ask that you please be responsible about what you choose to publish. Better yet, please contact the FBI and report where you got it.

4. The CIA or the White House wrote the "tell-all" book themselves.

We suspect that this has been done several times. In fact, we suspect that fully half to two-thirds of the "I was a CIA analyst/operative/janitor, and I'm revealing the inner workings of the Agency" books were written by the CIA or the White House for public relations.

Perhaps someone should ask why a spook organization would even have a public relations department. A bit of a paradox for a covert organization.

Nevertheless, intelligence organizations do have PR departments, and we suspect that their employees either write the books or work closely with the authors, who are often former analysts. Sometimes publishers knowingly cooperate with the PR publication, and sometimes publishers get buffaloed by their own willingness to publish a scoop no matter who gets hurt.

We know what you're thinking . . . Why would the CIA or the White House write a "tell-all" book themselves?

"American spy and military books are terrorists' handbooks." ~ Jay Holmes

---

The CIA knows and understands this well. Every country has intelligence teams that study the novels and the "tell-all" books of other countries. As authors, we only hope most of those countries are paying cash for the books and not pirating them like China does. Terrorist organizations, along with their clones and wannabes, are also well aware of the benefits to be gleaned from printed information. An easy way to misinform terrorists and foreign countries is to let them "discover" the information for themselves in a publication.

What the White House knows and understands well is the power of propaganda. "Information" that makes the administration look good is so much more believable if it comes from an "independent" source that is "revealing secrets" than it is coming from a White House press conference.

Every time a book claims to be slipping under the CIA/Pentagon radar to expose the "real story," you can lay odds there is something in that book that supports the administration's agenda, and that the administration knows all about it long before it hits the presses. Seriously. If there's an advance release copy under the arm of every journalist in Georgetown and the Pentagon is whining that it hasn't seen the manuscript, it's quite likely a public relations campaign.

Bottom Line: When someone walks in wearing the "I'm A Spy" T-shirt with a "tell-all" book, ask some questions about them, their motivations, and your own.

Writing Tip: If you ever write a scene like this, where Jason Bond Smiley is pimping his "tell-all" book, feel free to make it a comic scene in which Smiley is the brunt of the joke. You won't offend anyone in the IC.

9
INTELLIGENCE AGENCIES—WHAT, TO WHOM, AND WHERE?

ONE OF THE MOST COMMON MISTAKES IN FICTION IS CONFUSING which intelligence agencies have the power to do what, to whom, and where they have the authority to do it. While a veritable plethora of military and civilian intelligence organizations exist, we'll focus on the four biggest branches, which are also the ones most commonly assigned imaginative extracurricular activities by fiction authors: the Central Intelligence Agency ("CIA" or "the Company"), the Federal Bureau of Investigation ("FBI"), the Department of Homeland Security ("DHS"), and the National Security Agency/Central Security Service ("NSA/CSS" or "NSA"). Throughout this section, we will also highlight the very realistic sources of conflict for fictional characters.

"If prostitution is the world's oldest profession, espionage is the second oldest profession." ~ Old Espionage Adage

CENTRAL INTELLIGENCE AGENCY—a.k.a. CIA, The Company

ORIGINS

Espionage in the United States dates back to the days of General Washington and the American Revolution. Washington's staff and the Continental Congress conducted espionage operations against the British, both in America and in Europe. At various times after the revolution, we have not had a standing Army, but we did have a small standing Navy. The Navy, therefore, was the obvious choice for finding out what was going on in the rest of the world, but it did not have extensive resources for intelligence.

To fill that gap prior to WWII, there was an "old boy network" operating—a casual private network of like-minded individuals devoted to the interests of the nation. This casual network was more active during some periods and less active during others. Some claim it was a "deep state" Masonic collaboration, but we don't ascribe to that theory. What we do know is that one period this network was extremely active was during the 1930s as war raged in Europe and Hitler's powers grew. But there aren't any records or any specifics beyond whispered anecdote and reason. Secrecy was paramount in the network.

If all of this is a bit cloudy, that's because that's how the old boy network wanted it. After all, though a handful of congressmen may have been aware of their efforts, the men and women involved in the network weren't exactly turning in reports to the House and the Senate. As a result, history cannot with any certainty record anything except, "There was a network." It makes for short history books.

By 1934, five years before Hitler invaded Czechoslovakia and seven years before Pearl Harbor, a man named William "Wild Bill" Donovan was at the center of those substantial old boy network efforts. Donovan, America's "Father of Central Intelligence," was an attorney and a WWI Army officer. He went on to become the director of the Office of Strategic Services ("OSS"), which was America's principal foreign intelligence service during the Second World War. By the end of WWII, the Soviet threat had grown to the point that the United States had a continuing, urgent need for foreign intelligence. On September 18, 1947, President Harry Truman signed the charter founding the Central Intelligence Agency, which was created as an intelligence organization that all others should report to in order to "centralize" our intelligence efforts.

PURPOSE

If novels, TV, and the mainstream media are to be believed, the CIA exists to break serial killers out of jail for the purpose of controlling Mexican drug lords and to kidnap small children for mind-control experiments that rip open the space/time continuum. In reality, the purpose of the CIA is to collect, assess, and disseminate intelligence on foreign individuals and countries. It also has a Clandestine Operations Division.

JURISDICTION

CIA jurisdiction is almost entirely restricted to foreign soil. Any exceptions to this are highly limited and usually quite specific in their scope, such as placing a counterterrorism specialist with the New York City Police Department for the specific purpose of supporting police counterterrorism efforts. According to CIA leadership, the CIA *never* runs its own operations on American soil.

Entire novels and TV series are premised on the notion that the CIA conducts elaborate surveillance and deep-cover operations involving American citizens on American soil (i.e., *Homeland, Legends,* and *Burn Notice*). No. Even in the case of an internal investigation, the agency must contact the FBI and/or the DHS as soon as surveillance or action on American soil is involved. This applies even if it is one of the Company's own. The classic example of that fact is the surveillance and apprehension of Cold War traitor Aldrich Ames.

Ames held a variety of positions at the CIA, both domestically and abroad during the course of his career, including serving as a desk officer on the Soviet desk at CIA Headquarters. He was also a mole for the Soviets. When he took a field assignment in Italy, he suddenly began to look suspiciously wealthy for a government employee, and he attracted CIA attention. While he was in Italy the CIA was free to watch him. Suspicions deepened.

Ames was brought back to DC and reassigned to the Soviet desk, but this time with limited access. The CIA kept an eye on his work internally just long enough to confirm its suspicions. At that point the Company called in the FBI. The FBI conducted comprehensive surveillance on Ames and caught him red-handed selling information to Russia. The FBI arrested him in February 1994, and he is still in jail to this day serving a life sentence in a federal prison in Allentown, Pennsylvania.

Hollywood would have had the CIA kill Aldrich Ames. Plenty of CIA officers would line up for the chance to play out that fiction to this day if it were true that the CIA goes after American citizens on American soil. The fact that Ames is still alive at all and sucking off of the US taxpayers he betrayed for his continued parasitic existence is proof that it doesn't.

One reason the CIA strictly adheres to the tenet of not running operations on US soil is because it is careful to avoid any legal entanglements with US federal judges. The Company doesn't like conversations with federal judges. The number of conversations with US federal judges that it has budgeted each year is always zero. As long as the United States has a strong judicial system, that won't change.

If CIA operatives *were* ever to be caught surveilling an American on American soil, it would be considered an extreme breach. The president would become involved and would most likely turn the case over to the attorney general.

That doesn't mean that the Company doesn't skate the razor's edge of the law at times. For example, the CIA has been known to recruit visitors to the United States, but even that must be done very delicately. If the recruitment target at any point feels they have been spied upon, it's considered a violation of their rights rather than a recruitment.

US military bases pose a fine line for this "exclusively foreign soil" rule. If the foreign national is visiting on a US military base, that individual already has an established relationship with the United States. The CIA would be expanding on that preexisting relationship rather than creating a new one. Even then, the Company would co-opt the person who extended the invitation to that foreign national and ask that person to promote the relationship instead of the CIA doing it directly.

If the foreign national is visiting the United States from China or another hostile nation, they will be expecting some attempt to recruit them, and their country will be watching closely. Because of that, a visit to the military base is not the best time to approach that person. However, as a general rule, most foreign nationals visiting US military bases are from our allied countries, and we don't really want to spy on them much anyway. The United States prefers to set up mutually beneficial relationships with our allies in which people volunteer information, and no spying is necessary.

A factor to consider is that the US military has its own spy apparatus, and it doesn't need the CIA or FBI to be involved. The CIA sometimes picks things up the long way around. For example, if the CIA finds out from a double agent in Russia that one of our Army people is giving away secrets, the Company would turn over that case to the Army. The Army would put counterintelligence on it, gather evidence, and get the Criminal Investigation Division ("CID") involved. The CID is also the agency that would investigate other crimes by military personnel, whether those personnel are on a base or off base in a foreign country.

Another case for potential CIA involvement would be if a target is on a base in a foreign country and committing an espionage crime. In that instance, the CIA might quietly snatch up the spy when he's off the base. That would give the opportunity for the CIA and the military branch to play Good Cop/Bad Cop.

The target would not know that the CIA had already talked to the Army and the CID. The CIA and the CID would present themselves to the suspect as being in opposition to each other. Usually, the CIA would play the good cop because the CIA doesn't prosecute anyone. The CID, on the other hand, does prosecute people, and it can pursue the death penalty in a court-martial.

In some cases, the CIA might be interested in getting information from the suspect or in "turning" him—making him a double agent. If so, the CIA might offer to save the suspect from a military court-martial and get them into a federal civil court. However, even if a suspect takes a civil plea bargain, if they screw up that plea bargain at any point in the future, they can still be prosecuted in a military court. There is no statute of limitations in the military for espionage charges.

Conflict Alert: This can be a rich source for pissing matches between your characters. Jurisdiction and duties are fuzzy and overlapping between the FBI and the DHS on American soil. Please, though, if characters do engage in pissing matches over jurisdiction of spies and terrorists on American soil, leave the CIA out of it.

So how does the CIA know whether to contact the FBI or the DHS when a target under surveillance travels to the US?

That depends on whether the target individual is suspected of being a spy, a terrorist, or both. According to *Merriam-Webster*, a spy is one who tries to secretly obtain information about a country, organization, etc. A terrorist is one who uses violence or intimidation in pursuit of a political goal. Technically, the FBI is tasked with the prevention of intelligence gathering and with the surveillance and apprehension of spies. This is known as "counterintelligence." Technically, the DHS is tasked with the prevention of terrorist activities and with the surveillance and apprehension of terrorists. This is known as "counterterrorism." The reality is a bit more complicated.

Let's look at some examples:

1. The CIA has been watching Professor Sergei Putavich, a Russian national, in the backstreets of Amsterdam. Putavich comes to America to teach classes on cultural sensitivity at UC Davis. The CIA suspects that Sergei intends to spy and to recruit spies on the campus, but it does not think he has any intention to either plan or execute a terrorist act. Putavich's perceived goals fall under the umbrella of counterintelligence. The FBI is responsible for domestic counterintelligence. Therefore, the CIA would inform both the FBI and the DHS.

Wait. What? Both? ... Please bear with us.

2. Achmed Mohammed, born in Lansing, Michigan, to Iraqi parents, travels to Pakistan to join the radical Islamic terrorist flavor of the day and catches the attention of the CIA. Achmed travels home. He is an American citizen suspected of plotting terrorist acts against America, which falls under the auspices of counterterrorism. The DHS is responsible for handling domestic counterterrorism. Therefore, the CIA would inform both the FBI and the DHS.

3. The CIA is keeping an eye on Alhaji Ibrahim in Nigeria, who is in charge of public works in Borno State and is suspected of thick ties to Boko Haram. Ibrahim, a Nigerian national, travels to America for an international conference on terrorism in Houston. The CIA is not certain if his intent is to gather intelligence or to plot a terrorist act. Suspicions require responses from both counterintelligence and counterterrorism, so the CIA contacts both the FBI and the DHS.

Ideally, the FBI handles counterintelligence and the DHS handles counterterrorism. In reality, the FBI has dedicated counterintelligence agents who are excellent at finding that one anomaly or inconsistency that allows them to catch spies and moles. However, also in reality, the team is practically orphaned in the Bureau, and it is traditionally not well supported. The DHS, while primarily focused on counterterrorism, also has counterintelligence personnel. It's all about as well-defined as the US tax code, and there are several overlaps. As a result, in all cases, the CIA covers its own butt by notifying both the FBI and the DHS when surveillance targets come to American shores, and it stands back and lets those two organizations duke it out for jurisdiction.

Are you confused yet? Don't worry. So is everyone else. The one thing that is certain is that if a target comes to America, that target is no longer in the CIA's jurisdiction.

Conflict Alert: Have FBI characters caught in a pissing match with DHS characters for jurisdiction over a case the CIA has turned over to both organizations.

SCOPE OF OPERATIONS

The CIA is authorized to gather intelligence on foreign countries and individuals outside of the United States and to conduct clandestine operations in foreign countries.

To accomplish its goals, the CIA can use its own employees, a.k.a. "blue badgers" because they carry blue badges, contractors, known because of their green badges as "green badgers," or foreign agents. Any operation can consist of any combination of these individuals. However, employees and contractors are not usually on the same mission together in the field. Contractors do report to the CIA, but in the field, they generally keep their distance from blue badgers for their own insulation and security concerns. Blue badgers in the field keep their distance from contractors for the same reasons.

ARRESTING AUTHORITY

The CIA does *not* have the authority to arrest anyone. While at times the CIA may detain foreigners in the process of covert actions, it does not arrest those individuals, and it never detains people for the purpose of prosecution in a legal system. No one detained by the CIA, unless later arrested by some other organization, appears in the American legal system. To arrest someone on foreign soil for the purpose of prosecution, the CIA must cooperate with the FBI, which in turn must cooperate with the host country where the target is located.

An example of this agency interaction is the arrest of the first World Trade Center bomber, Ramzi Yousef, in Islamabad, Pakistan.

On February 26, 1993, Ramzi Yousef and his coconspirators detonated a van full of explosives in the parking garage underneath the World Trade Center in New York City. Their intent was to blast the North Tower into the South Tower to bring them both down. They failed in their goal, but they did kill six people and injure over one thousand. Ramzi Yousef escaped from the United States, and the worldwide hunt was on.

A US State Department employee got the idea that some good old-fashioned, low budget HUMINT ("Human Intelligence") could be productive in the search for Ramzi Yousef. The State Department employee thought a trick he had used before could be useful, so he ran it past the State Department. Some folks at State pooh-poohed the idea, saying it wouldn't work, and were dead set against it. Some at State didn't want to do it because they thought it would be insulting to Muslims. This gentleman, however, was terminally ill and at the end of his career and life. He could have accepted medical disability and retired, but instead, he stayed in the field in Pakistan and implemented his idea in spite of opposition.

He passed out thousands of matchbooks printed with a wanted ad for Ramzi Yousef that included a reward for $2,000,000 USD and contact information for the State Department security team in Pakistan. He left these matchbooks at hotels, restaurants, gas stations, etc., for the owners and employees to pass out. His strategy produced a viable lead.

Front Cover of Ramzi Yousef Matchbook
Image by Former CIA Officer Doug Patteson*

At that point, the US State Department turned over the lead to the CIA. The CIA located Yousef in Islamabad and kept him under surveillance until an FBI team could arrive in Pakistan. The FBI coordinated with the Pakistan government for Yousef's arrest. The FBI executed the raid, apprehended Yousef, brought him out of the building where he was hiding, and delivered him to the Islamabad Police, who were waiting outside during the raid. The Islamabad Police performed the arrest and immediately turned him back to the FBI team. The FBI team brought Yousef back to New York for formal prosecution.

Writing Tip: The hunt for Ramzi Yousef was before the days of the DHS. If you would prefer that your CIA characters interact with the DHS to apprehend modern-day suspects overseas, the DHS can also coordinate with foreign governments to bring in criminals. They would do so in the same manner as the FBI.

OVERSIGHT

If you believe TV, books, movies, Facebook posts, "news" media, any president, or anyone in Congress, the CIA is a rogue organization that is funded from thin air and hides its activities from everyone on the planet, especially the US president and Congress. In reality, the CIA reports to the Director of National Intelligence, who reports to the president, and the agency is overseen by the Senate and House Permanent Select Committees on Intelligence.

We know what you're thinking . . . Wait! What, exactly, are the Senate and House Permanent Select Committees on Intelligence?

There are both a Senate Permanent Select Committee on Intelligence and a House Permanent Select Committee on Intelligence. The political makeup of these committees is determined by the political makeup of the Senate and of the House, respectively. In other words, the controlling party in each legislative body has the controlling majority and the chairmanship on its respective committee. This political recipe changes every two years with each election. The membership of the committees also changes as committee members step down from the committees.

We know. . . . That sounds like quite a bit of shifting about. In fact, we'd say the one constant of the committees and their members is that anything they approve that becomes unpopular with their constituents will be blamed on the CIA, the NSA, or the DHS. (See the Life Cycle of Controversial Practices later in this section.)

The members of the committees are chosen by their respective parties. As with any group of politicians, some of these committee members are consistently good at defending the country, while some are consistently good at defending their own political interests. And that is all we will say about that.

Any legislation pertaining to intelligence operations passes through these committees before it is presented to the House or Senate, and there must be a quorum of committee members present for that review. The committees also review more of the classified details concerning intelligence funding than the rest of Congress gets to see.

No one gets rich working for the government unless they are a president or a member of Congress. CIA and other IC employees certainly don't. It is guaranteed that none of them woke up this morning and said, "Hey. Let's all empty our bank accounts so we can set up a black site in the Arctic and waterboard people for fun." Every controversial practice in operation has to be funded, and funding requires Congress and the president. In other words, the CIA has *never* operated without oversight from Congress and the White House.

We know this might cause some confusion since every president seems to be perpetually surprised at what goes on in the Intelligence Community, and Congress swears it has never heard of any of the controversial practices within the IC. Disavowing knowledge of controversial intelligence programs is a favorite ploy of politicians. It's especially easy for politicians to blame the CIA for the politicians' own mistakes and for any programs that prove to be unpopular with their constituents. That's because politicians all know the CIA will keep its mouth shut. That's what the CIA does. We'll spell it out...

THE LIFE CYCLE OF CONTROVERSIAL PRACTICES

1. The CIA proposes an operation to the president and the congressional committees.

2. Congressional committees approve it, sometimes with unbridled enthusiasm and their best Rambo imitations.

3. The president signs off on it, and the program is funded.

4. The CIA implements the program.

5. The media "discovers" some element of the program and exposes it to the public, usually with only partial information and a great deal of assumption and speculation passed off as fact. This "discovery" is often prompted by a large explosion or two somewhere on the planet.

6. The public is horrified.

7. Media rakes in the cash by spinning things up as much as it can.

8. Politicians pretend the CIA is off on some rogue tangent and that Congress and the president will champion the people by getting the agency back on track.

9. The congressional committee members who were first to endorse the program do everything they can to distance themselves from it, up to and including calling for special hearings and prosecution of the CIA operatives who implemented their orders.

10. The CIA spooks hold a barbecue and laugh about it. They've seen this a hundred times before. If they weren't capable of laughing about it, they would all go insane or commit suicide.

11. Something new happens, often including an explosion or two somewhere on the planet, and Congress blames the CIA for not preventing it.

12. Congressional committee members transform back into Rambo and demand action, wanting heads to roll and bodies to fly.

13. Return to step one. Wash, rinse, repeat.

Operatives attain emotional resolution with this cycle without violence by reminding themselves that there is a long line of self-serving politicians waiting to replace whichever self-serving politician is most annoying at any given moment.

Waterboarding is an excellent example of this Life Cycle of Controversial Practices. Bayard & Holmes *cough, cough* heard a rumor *cough, cough* that the CIA adapted waterboarding for enhanced interrogations to give Congress something it could sign off on without feeling too squeamish. In the post-9/11 atmosphere, the members of Congress openly brandished their Rambo knives and were eager to be the first to be known for doing whatever it took to save the country from Islamic terrorists. Waterboarding was specifically approved by the White House, the Secretary of State, and the Department of Justice in 2002, and Congress was informed at that time. Then the American public wrapped itself in the Patriot Act, declared "Mission Accomplished," and moved on while the CIA and the military implemented measures to once more keep the perpetual fight from our shores.

Years later, the media "discovered" waterboarding and a deep well of cash to be made. Congress "forgot" that it signed off on the practice and shouted its outrage about that naughty CIA. The media industry rejoiced, and much money was made by all.

We'll let you search on your own to find out which senators and representatives squealed loudest and did the most aggressive finger-pointing. That will tell you who had the best Rambo costumes in the days after 9/11.

Bottom Line: As much as the president and Congress like to pretend otherwise, the CIA does nothing that is not funded by Congress and signed off on by the president.

THE COLD WAR NICARAGUAN SEA MINING OPERATION

Another great example of this Life Cycle of Controversial Practices was the CIA's sea mining operation in Nicaraguan coastal waters during the 1980s. In the thick of the Cold War, Nicaraguan president Daniel Ortega was solidly in the Soviet camp—a puppet of the Soviet Union. The goal of the Soviets and Cubans was to install similar Soviet puppet governments in El Salvador, Honduras, and Guatemala. To achieve this goal, the Soviets and Cubans were smuggling weapons into Nicaragua in ships from neutral countries and transporting them to Sandinista-clone communist rebels in surrounding countries. The CIA, tasked with keeping the Soviet Union out of Central America, wanted to stop these smuggled weapons, or at least to make it far more difficult for the Soviets and Cubans to arm the Sandinistas.

The CIA proposed a program in which it would seed Nicaraguan coastal waters with mines made from local materials for the purpose of doing minimal damage to cargo ships coming into the country. President Reagan was not willing to approve the operation without Congress being on board.

Congressional intelligence committees immediately objected. They saw no purpose in inflicting minimal damage. They were concerned that the operation would not be worthwhile unless the United States blew ships completely out of the water. With some effort, the CIA convinced the congressional committees that there was no need to sink the ships of neutral countries to achieve their goal. Congress approved and funded the operation, and Reagan signed off on it.

CIA-backed operatives seeded the Nicaraguan coastal waters with sea mines made from local materials to make it look like a sad local attempt to sink ships. A Norwegian ship bumped into one, and the mine did minimal damage. No one was endangered by the blast, just as the CIA had planned. Also, as the CIA had estimated, maritime insurance rates went through the roof overnight for ships bound to Nicaragua. Ships from neutral countries could no longer profit from traveling to Nicaragua. Soviets and Cubans were forced to smuggle arms to the Sandinistas and Sandinista-clones in their own vessels, making them much easier for the CIA to monitor and intercept. This helped the CIA achieve the important goal of preventing more Soviet puppet regimes from springing up in Central America.

It eventually came out that the CIA was behind the sea mining of the Nicaraguan shores. The media, always alert for something that will outrage the public into buying their product and never particularly concerned with accuracy, jumped right on it. Media characterized the program as a CIA screwup because no serious damage was done to any ships. Apparently, the media was not aware that we have a US Navy that could have blasted everything in the Nicaraguan harbor into flotsam. The public, still sour from the Vietnam War, complied and became profitably outraged. Congress claimed to be shocked and sickened by the operation, conveniently forgetting that it not only approved the operation, but that some of its committee members had wanted to actually sink ships from neutral countries.

Bottom Line: If a member or former member of a Congress is making a public fuss about something the CIA is doing or has done, you can pretty well bet that congressman was the first to "go Rambo," and now they are trying to distance themselves. This is standard operating procedure for Congress. The media industry *loves* it when congressmen get their self-righteous on because it makes the media industry's job of getting its profits on very easy.

Conflict Alert: The natural and realistic dynamic between the CIA and Congress, some presidents, and the media is a rich source for conflict for your fictional characters, as it is in real life.

---

*Doug Patteson is a former CIA officer with extensive overseas experience. He is skilled in several foreign languages, personal security, tactical driving, counter terrorism tactics, and small arms. He holds an MBA from Wharton and has worked in high tech, private equity, and manufacturing. He regularly writes on business and intelligence topics for both web and print publications. And if that's not enough cool for you, he's also an executive producer of *Texas Zombie Wars: Dallas*.

Doug is a contributor to Inglorious Amateurs, which is a site created by former CIA intelligence officers to give readers a timely and informed look at intelligence and related matters. You can find Doug on Twitter at @GrayManActual and at the Inglorious Amateurs website at https://www.ingloriousamateurs.com. We highly recommend both the website and the quality gear from their online shop.

Thank you again for the pictures, Doug, and all the best to you, Texas Zombie Wars, and the Inglorious Amateurs.

FEDERAL BUREAU OF INVESTIGATION—a.k.a. FBI ORIGINS

This section about the origins of the FBI is substantially longer than that of the other intelligence organizations we cover here.

This speaks volumes about the FBI right up front—pun intended. It's not because the FBI has a longer history, but that the history it does have is open and available. That's because the FBI, unlike the CIA or the NSA, is a law enforcement body focused on the investigation, apprehension, and prosecution of criminals.

When an agency is focused on prosecution, its methods and procedures are discussed openly in courtrooms. While the FBI certainly has plenty of responsibilities and hardworking special agents, the Bureau simply doesn't rack up secrets at the same rate the other intelligence organizations do. More of their history is available to the public, and it always has been.

Criminal law and its enforcement is traditionally left to individual states. However, at the turn of the twentieth century, the United States was literally united from coast to coast due to advances in transportation and communication. In turn, corruption and criminal syndicates also spread from coast to coast using those same advances. Local and state law enforcement entities were not empowered to keep up with these criminal activities and organizations once crooks had the ability to easily cross out of jurisdictional reach. Our country needed a federal investigative and law enforcement body to keep pace with changing times and changing technology.

In 1908, US Attorney General Charles Bonaparte had a handful of full-time investigators in the Justice Department's Office of the Chief Examiner. They were primarily accountants who reviewed the financial transactions of the federal courts. Bonaparte sought and received authorization to build a more efficient investigative arm of the Justice Department for the purpose of investigating federal crimes. He recruited ten Secret Service agents out of retirement and made them special agents. They reported to Chief Examiner Stanley W. Finch for the first time on July 26, 1908. This date is considered the birthday of the Federal Bureau of Investigation, though it was not to carry that name quite yet. By March of 1909, the office had thirty-four agents and was renamed the Bureau of Investigation.

Many in government and in the public feared the Bureau's growing power for a number of reasons. First, those were wild and wooly days, and the rampant corruption and gang activity throughout the country was reflected by some of the same activities and behaviors in the Bureau. Second, law enforcement was not actually a recognized profession at that time, and law enforcement officers were more closely tied to political agendas rather than service to the nation. Third, the country was still largely rural, and people strongly valued their independence. A federal law enforcement body was highly controversial, as it was seen as infringing on the independent jurisdiction and powers of individual states. The Bureau had an uphill battle to win the "hearts and minds" of Congress and the public.

However, the same progress in transportation and communications that provided tools for criminals also allowed the fledgling investigative branch to thrive. It not only made it possible to police a federal territory, but it also made it feasible for the citizens of the United States to communicate and travel across long distances on a more regular basis. The public became more aware of and attuned to their position as part of a nation rather than just part of a town or a state. Public opinion became progressively more favorable toward a federal government and with it, a federal investigative and law enforcement branch.

By 1917, the Bureau had over three hundred special agents and as many support staff. It had field offices in major cities throughout America, as well as several along the Mexican border for the purpose of investigating smuggling and neutrality violations and collecting intelligence. Once America entered WWI, the Bureau also investigated draft dodgers, Espionage Act violators, and immigrants suspected of radicalism.

With the advent of the Prohibition years, followed by the Great Depression surge of interstate gang activity, numerous federal crime laws were passed. More federal laws meant more federal law enforcement, and the Bureau's powers were expanded. In the early 1930s, the Justice Department started redrawing and relabeling the organizational structure of the Bureau of Investigation in an effort to meet these growing demands. After a bit of experimentation, the Justice Department in 1935 settled on "Federal Bureau of Investigation" as the name of its agency that would encompass all of its federal investigators.

Backing up a bit to 1917 . . . In that year, the Bureau of Investigation hired a special agent by the name of J. Edgar Hoover, a young graduate of George Washington University Law School. Throughout WWI, Hoover headed the enemy alien operations and investigated suspected anarchists and communists. After the war, he led the charge against communists and the Industrial Workers of the World, a.k.a. the Wobblies, during the Red Scare years of 1919 and 1920. On May 10, 1924, Attorney General Harlan Fiske Stone appointed J. Edgar Hoover to head up the Bureau of Investigation. J. Edgar Hoover reigned over the Bureau for the next forty-eight years and through eight presidential administrations.

The early 1920s were an intense time in the world. The fledgling Communist Party of the Soviet Union saw opportunity to be grasped by creating political chaos—something the Soviets, a.k.a. Russians, still do to this day as frequently as they can. Communism was young, and so was the Soviet Union. The Soviet Union wasted no time in spreading its influence throughout the world in its mission to be the capital of world communism, and it focused much of its efforts in the United States. It was J. Edgar

Hoover's mission in life to keep that communist influence out. Numerous treatises about J. Edgar Hoover and his controversial methods of fighting communism on the domestic front populate library shelves and Amazon selections. This will not be one of them, as that specific aspect of FBI history is beyond the scope of this book.

Hoover began his work in 1924 by cleaning house. He fired any special agents he thought were unqualified, including two of the three women special agents in the Bureau. The third female special agent, Miss Lenore Houston, was asked to resign in 1928. It wasn't until 1972 that women once again served as special agents in the FBI. As of 2017, women still only comprised approximately 17 percent of the Bureau's special agent force.

At his beginning, Hoover also eliminated the seniority rule of promotion and established uniform performance appraisals. New agents were required to be between twenty-five and thirty-five years of age, preferably with a law or accounting background. Hoover also established regular inspections of headquarters and field offices. He did all of these for the purpose of professionalizing federal investigations and law enforcement.

Under his shepherding, his emphasis on professionalizing law enforcement grew and influenced policing nationwide. By 1926, law enforcement agencies across the country were contributing fingerprint cards to the Bureau's Identification Division for the creation of a federal criminal database. The Technical Laboratory was established in 1932 for research into forensics and criminology. In 1935, the FBI National Academy was established and began training police professionals from law enforcement agencies across the country in investigative techniques. By the 1940s, the National Academy was training police professionals from all over the world. The FBI had become the gold standard for professional police investigations, and many would say it still is today.

The FBI spent much of the 1930s repelling fascists and communists, as well as tending to human trafficking, interstate gangsters, and organized crime. When America was ramping up for WWII in 1940, Congress reestablished the draft, and the FBI added chasing down draft dodgers to its to-do list once more. On December 7, 1941, when the Japanese bombed Pearl Harbor, the FBI headquarters and its fifty-four field offices began twenty-four-hour schedules. War-related investigations ensued, and the FBI foiled sabotage plots and tracked foreign spies on US soil.

After the war, FBI focus—always in addition to investigating and enforcing federal criminal law—centered on the growing Soviet threat and the domestic challenge of fighting communists in America during the Cold War. In 1956, Hoover began a secret counterintelligence program known as "COINTELPRO" for the purpose of targeting the US Communist Party and its members. The program quickly expanded to be used to infiltrate and disrupt any group deemed to be radical by the American government. It is well known that the government initially considered Civil Rights Movement leaders to be radical, and J. Edgar Hoover's FBI kept surveillance on many, including Martin Luther King Jr. What is less known is that Hoover's FBI also kept a close eye on KKK leaders and other white supremacist organizations, as they were *also* considered to be radical.

The 1960s and the Civil Rights Movement led to yet another expansion of FBI powers and duties to include the enforcement of federal civil rights laws. Worth a special note is the Omnibus Crime Control and Safe Streets Act of 1968. This act provided for the use of court-ordered electronic surveillance in the investigation of certain specified violations. This was a powerful tool in the hands of the FBI. However, it may surprise people to learn that J. Edgar Hoover was not a defender of wiretapping and other intrusive surveillance techniques, and he forbade the FBI to use those techniques unless the special agents strictly followed the letter of the Omnibus Crime Control Act.

The Vietnam era saw the rise of the New Left, which was a broad counterculture movement that included a variety of people from peaceful protestors to violent terrorists such as the Weather Underground and the Symbionese Liberation Army. The New Left was known for its "romance with violence." Then, in 1970, the National Guard killed four unarmed students at Kent State University during a protest, and four New Left adherents blew up the Army Mathematics Research Center with a homemade bomb, killing one graduate and injuring three others. Suddenly that violence didn't seem quite so romantic. Most of the New Left brought it down a notch after that, but the Weathermen and their spin-offs continued. The FBI used both traditional investigative methods and the controversial COINTELPRO operations to target the New Left movement until Hoover discontinued COINTELPRO activities in April of 1971. The FBI itself says at its web site that "COINTELPRO was later rightfully criticized by Congress and the American people for abridging First Amendment rights and for other reasons."

J. Edgar Hoover died on May 2, 1972 at the age of seventy-seven, only eight days short of being director of the FBI for forty-eight years. After his death, Congress passed a law limiting the tenure of any future FBI director to a term of ten years.

Clarence Kelley, the Kansas City police chief, became the new director of the FBI on July 9, 1973, only three days before Nixon aides began stepping down in the wake of the Watergate scandal. It was revealed that the FBI had illegally protected Nixon from investigation. Congressional hearings ensued, and Attorney General Edward Levi established detailed guidelines for the FBI for the first time. Kelley fought to restore the Bureau's reputation as a professional law enforcement body and to build back the trust of the American people with a "Quality over Quantity" approach to investigations. The three national priorities of the FBI became set as foreign counterintelligence, organized crime, and white-collar crime.

As criminals and crime evolved, so did crime-fighting technologies. By the late 1970s, the Bureau had the ability to detect "latent" fingerprints that were virtually invisible. The Behavioral Analysis Unit—a household term thanks to *Criminal Minds*—was hard at work applying psychological methods of criminal profiling, and in 1984, the National Center for the Analysis of Violent Crime was established to further research and to provide services in identifying suspects and predicting criminal behavior to other law enforcement agencies across the country.

The fight against organized crime took on new dimensions in the 1980s with travel and communications technologies that allowed criminal and terrorist organizations—two siblings frequently joined at the hip—to operate on an international level. International terrorism became a thing, and in 1982, FBI Director William H. Webster made counterterrorism a fourth priority for the FBI. That same year, the Bureau was given concurrent jurisdiction with the DEA over the enforcement of federal narcotics laws. Counterintelligence efforts also paid off, and the FBI ferreted out so many moles in the US government during the mid-1980s that 1985 became known as "The Year of the Spy." (Refer to The Walker Family Spy Ring toward the end of this FBI section.) And in crime-fighting technology, the FBI began performing DNA analysis on criminal investigations in 1988.

On November 10, 1989, the Berlin Wall came down. The Soviet Union dissolved and began calling itself RUSSIA, or what we call the Reorganized Union of Soviet Socialists In Asia. With the fall of the Soviet Union, the Islamic mujahedeen who had been fighting them found themselves with too much time on their hands. They turned their eyes West, and the historical ebb and flow of Islamic terrorist ambitions began to take a new upswing.

Osama bin Laden, a wealthy Saudi businessman, began planning attacks on America and training followers. In 1993, Ramzi Yousef became the first bin Laden terrorist camp alum to attack Americans on American soil by planting a truck bomb in the parking garage of the World Trade Center. (Refer to Ramzi Yousef mentioned previously in the CIA section.) Osama bin Laden and Al-Qaeda followed up this attack with attacks on the US embassies in Kenya and Tanzania and on the USS *Cole*. The FBI was crucial in investigating the crime scenes, identifying victims, and determining that Al-Qaeda and bin Laden were behind the attacks.

Then, on September 11, 2001, Al-Qaeda agents flew planes into the Pentagon and the World Trade Center Twin Towers and brought them down, killing almost three thousand people. The FBI began the largest investigation of its history—and one of the Bureau's largest reorganizations, which once more expanded its powers. Before the attacks on 9/11, the FBI was completely focused on investigation and criminal *prosecution,* even in the case of terrorism. *Prevention* of terrorism was not particularly on the Bureau's radar. After 9/11, preventing terrorist attacks was moved to the top of the list of the ten priorities that guide the FBI to this date.

PURPOSE

The FBI was originally the federal government's investigative agency. Now, the FBI investigates both criminal and terrorist activities and has offices in several overseas US embassies. Its official priorities are listed at the FBI web site:

1. Protect the United States from terrorist attack

2. Protect the United States against foreign intelligence operations and espionage
3. Protect the United States against cyber-based attacks and high-technology crimes
4. Combat public corruption at all levels
5. Protect civil rights
6. Combat transnational/national criminal organizations and enterprises
7. Combat major white-collar crime
8. Combat significant violent crime
9. Support federal, state, local, and international partners
10. Upgrade technology to successfully perform the FBI's mission

Unofficially, the FBI is tasked with keeping Jos. A. Banks in business selling suits. The straightlaced G-man image is quite accurate with the FBI. For example, it wasn't until the 1990s that the Bureau would even consider hiring someone who had experimented with marijuana, and then only if it was once or twice and very long ago.

> *"The FBI is very careful to avoid hiring people with criminal tendencies. The CIA is very careful to find and hire people with criminal tendencies."* ~ Jay Holmes

JURISDICTION

The FBI operates inside the United States as both an investigative and a law enforcement agency. Outside the United States, the FBI assists foreign governments in investigations and conducts investigations of crimes against Americans and against American installations. It also acts as a liaison to foreign law enforcement agencies.

SCOPE OF OPERATIONS

The FBI is authorized to conduct law enforcement and surveillance inside the United States. Outside the United States, it relies on the CIA for surveillance and must obtain the permission and cooperation of foreign governments for any US law enforcement activities on their territory. For example, in the Ramzi Yousef situation above, the FBI had to obtain the permission and cooperation of Pakistan to detain Yousef and to deliver him back to the United States for prosecution.

The FBI is primarily a law enforcement body, tracking down suspects after crimes are committed. As a result, undercover operations are not as large a slice of the FBI pie as they are of the CIA pie. However, FBI agents do go undercover at times. Historically, Agent Joe Pistone's outstanding work undercover as Donnie Brasco forever changed the FBI on that score.

In 1976, New York was plagued with Mafia truck hijackings. Agent Joseph Dominick "Joe" Pistone posed as a modestly successful jewel thief named Donnie Brasco and went undercover for what was supposed to be six months to infiltrate the fences who were moving the stolen goods from the hijackings. That assignment lasted over five years as "Donnie Brasco" quickly rose through the Bonanno Mafia family ranks under the sponsorship of thirty-year Mafia foot soldier Benjamin "Lefty" Ruggiero.

During that time, Pistone only saw his wife and children three or four times each year, and only for a day or two each time. He was also assigned four contract killings, which he handled by either manipulating himself out of the hit or working with the FBI to stage the killings. Over the course of his amazing undercover work, he collected evidence that led to over two hundred indictments and one hundred convictions. Pistone and his family still live in a secret location with assumed identities.

Pistone's undercover work opened up the deep-cover possibilities for the FBI. For the FBI's side, undercover work became more of a norm, and the Bureau has excellent agents in the field. Also, in what many see as a beneficial side effect of Pistone's work, the Mafia, upon finding out it had been so thoroughly infiltrated, went into overdrive killing each other. Win/win.

ARRESTING AUTHORITY

The FBI has the authority to arrest people anywhere within American jurisdiction. Outside of American jurisdiction, the FBI must obtain the cooperation of foreign governments. Those foreign entities make the actual arrest of the FBI targets and then turn them over to the Bureau agents for the purpose of prosecution.

Anyone arrested by the FBI or brought back to America by the FBI for the purpose of prosecution will appear in the American federal court system, and they will have all of the rights and protections of anyone arrested by any American police body. In other words, if the FBI picks you up, you won't be going to any secret prisons or Guantánamo.

OVERSIGHT

The FBI is a division of the Department of Justice. The director of the FBI is a political appointee who answers to another political appointee, the attorney general, who answers to the president. Congressional committees provide oversight for the Bureau, and the president also can and does speak directly to the Bureau.

Conflict Alert: The fact that the director of the FBI and the attorney general are political appointments can be a great source of conflict for your characters. In real life, many fine FBI agents become frustrated and angry when those at the top of the Bureau get caught up in political games that can compromise the agents' work and the reputation of the Bureau. There have also been cases where an attorney general and/or an FBI director left over from an administration change have been known to work against a new president.

THE FBI CASE EVERY WELL-EDUCATED PERSON SHOULD KNOW: THE WALKER FAMILY SPY RING

John Walker was a US Navy communications technician warrant officer. In October of 1967, Walker entered the Soviet Embassy in DC carrying high-end US Navy documents, including a cipher-key list. The Soviets always suspected walk-ins of being bogus, calling them "well-wishers." However, they verified some of the cipher-key list from another source and determined Walker was likely for real. In fact, the Soviets were so impressed with Walker's delivery that they contacted KGB Rezident Boris A. Solomatin, the station chief. If you watch *The Americans,* Solomatin was the Arkady Ivanovich.

Solomatin had never before spoken to a walk-in in person—KGB rezidents don't like to give themselves away like that. However, Solomatin was so impressed with the documents Walker brought in that he took a chance and personally interviewed the sailor. Walker reportedly offered to spy as a strictly business arrangement with no pretense of loving communism. Solomatin, intimately familiar with communism, found this to be highly credible and gave Walker several thousand dollars on the spot.

Solomatin never again met with Walker personally, but the Soviet Union awarded Solomatin the Order of the Red Banner for recruiting Walker and gave him a promotion to deputy chief of intelligence.

Solomatin assigned a handler to Walker, who set up dead drops throughout the DC area where the Soviets and Walker could exchange cash and information. A long-term romance between John Walker and the Soviet Union began, with Walker feeding the Soviets operational orders, war plans, technical manuals, and intelligence digests. The relationship lasted over twenty years, expanded to Walker's wife, brother, son, and friend, and compromised countless US operations, procedures, and operatives.

At the time Walker first approached the Soviets, he was married to a woman named Barbara, who had a propensity for drinking too much and cuckolding Walker with his fellow sailors. Walker had opened a bar in South Carolina and put Barbara in charge of it in the hopes that she would get clean and stop screwing sailors. She knew Walker was spying for the Soviet Union, and she accompanied him to dead drops and meetings. Her motive, like his, was cash. Barbara continued to drink and screw sailors, and the two divorced in 1976. The Soviets always viewed her as the weakest link in the Walker espionage chain. Any self-respecting Hollywood Soviets, such as the Jennings couple in *The Americans*, would have killed her off.

Walker's first recruit to his espionage ring was his friend and fellow US Navy radioman Senior Chief Petty Officer Jerry Whitworth. By 1975, the year Walker retired from the US Navy, Whitworth was actively spying for him. Whitworth clandestinely photographed documents, working in a van provided by the Soviets that he kept in a parking lot near his work at the Naval Communications Center Alameda.

John turned his older brother Arthur, as well, who had been a radioman and a retired US Navy lieutenant commander. After serving in the Navy, Arthur fell on hard times with a failed car radio business and went to work for a defense contractor in shipbuilding repair. Arthur provided John and the Soviets with war ship repair records and damage-control manuals.

One of Walker's three daughters, Laura Walker Snyder, served in the US Army. In an attempt at introducing a new father/daughter bonding activity, Walker approached her about joining him in his espionage activities in 1979. She refused. Instead, she discussed his proposition with her mother, only to find out that Barbara had known almost from the start. Over the years, Laura nagged her mother to rat out her father to the FBI, but Barbara was reluctant to do so. It is likely she was still receiving a share of the bounty from Walker.

When Walker had first approached the Soviets, his son, Michael Walker, was still a little boy. By 1983, that little boy had grown up to join the US Navy and was yeoman working in the administration office of the nuclear aircraft carrier USS *Nemitz*. During some no doubt poignant father/son talk, John Walker recruited his son to be a Soviet spy. Michael's contributions to the Soviet Cold War effort included material on weapon systems, nuclear weapons control, command procedures, hostile identification and stealth methods, and contingency target lists.

Over the years, the Pentagon and the US Navy suspected there were leaks. They had caught some of those leaks, but they knew there were more. During the course of those same years, Jerry Whitworth seemed to develop a bit of a conscience. In 1984, he started sending anonymous letters to the FBI office in San Francisco telling them there was a spy ring. He signed the letters "RUS." If Whitworth had "come in from the cold" at that point, he could have given up John and Michael Walker and plead out of the whole thing, but he never did. He stayed on the fence.

The next of the Walker ring to fall was ex-wife Barbara. In Holmes's suspicions, Walker made the mistake of taking Barbara's silence for granted and cut off her flow of money. Whether that happened or some other reason arose, Barbara decided to turn in her ex in November of 1984. She contacted the FBI Boston field office.

A special agent from Hyannis went out to interview her. When he arrived, Barbara was three sheets to the wind. She drank vodka throughout the interview and raged against John, all of which made her story suspect at best. Though her descriptions of contacts, exchanges, and dead drops were consistent with KGB techniques, the FBI agent noted that Barbara was a well-experienced drunk and decided it was all too wild—just a revenge call. He filed it away.

A month later, the agent's boss was doing a routine audit of closed cases. He read the report of Barbara's interview, and though he agreed with the agent that it was probably a revenge move, he decided to keep an eye on it. He called the Norfolk FBI office to discuss the report and sent a hard copy by fax. An agent in Norfolk, Robert Hunter, thought enough of the report to take it to his boss. The Norfolk agent's boss looked it over and called the DC office. In early March of 1985, the DC office authorized a full investigation under the code name Windflyer. Robert Hunter was told to go for it.

Hunter began by interviewing Barbara more seriously. She again described the contacts, the exchanges, and the dead drops, and her details were again consistent with KGB techniques. The agent then went to daughter Laura Walker Snyder, and she corroborated parts of her mother's story and actively cooperated with the FBI. The FBI tapped Walker's phones. Meanwhile, the US Naval Criminal Investigative Service spoke with hundreds of Walker's former Navy acquaintances.

On the night of May 19, 1985, the FBI followed John Walker to Partnership Road in Poolesville, Maryland, where John stood by a tree with a No Hunting sign. It was a dead drop. An hour later, the FBI confiscated 127 classified documents that John had left there—documents from the USS *Nimitz* that John's son had copied and sent to him. Soviet diplomat Aleksey Gavrilovich Tkachenko was spotted nearby, but he never made a move toward the tree to pick up the dummy bag left there by the FBI. Four hours later, in the early morning of May 20, the FBI arrested John Walker. Meanwhile, agents from the US Navy and the FBI were traveling to the USS *Nimitz*. They arrested twenty-two-year-old Michael Walker on May 22, and he confessed right there on the ship. Arthur Walker was arrested seven days later, and Jerry Whitworth turned himself in on June 3.

The thing the FBI does best is turn a case into a prosecution. It's what's upmost in their thinking from the moment a case is born, and the Bureau is meticulous in its handling of witnesses and suspects. Agents are skilled at avoiding compromising prosecution and at maneuvering witnesses and suspects. They keep their cases clean. Because of this, the US Navy sat back and let the FBI take the lead in the Walker Family Spy Ring case.

After being arrested, the Walkers could have been court-martialed through the US Navy, or they could have been prosecuted in civil courts by the FBI and still court-martialed through the US Navy. Military law does not have any statute of limitations on treason, and military courts are not limited by double jeopardy. That means a person can be tried and acquitted in civilian criminal court and still tried and convicted in a court-martial. They can also be convicted in criminal court, serve their time, and then be prosecuted again by a military court to do more time. US Navy prosecution, having a special hard spot in its heart for traitors, would have gone hard for both Walker and his son.

The FBI held out civil prosecution, and John Walker, far more afraid of the US Navy and its death penalty, plead out in criminal court. Many people close to the case believe he did this to protect his son, Michael, from a court-martial.

In the course of the prosecution, the FBI showed John Walker that he could both shift some of the blame to Whitworth and help out Michael if he cooperated. John went for it. As a result, Michael Walker was sentenced to only twenty-five years in federal prison and paroled in 2000 after serving fifteen years. Jerry Whitworth, on the other hand, received the heaviest sentence at 365 years. At the time of the writing of this book, Whitworth is still doing time in the US Penitentiary in Atwater, California. Arthur Walker received three life sentences plus forty years and died in prison in July 2014. John Walker, the man who organized the spy ring and sold America out to the Soviets for eighteen years, received only a life sentence. He died in prison in August 2014 at age seventy-seven. He would have been eligible for parole in May 2015.

DEPARTMENT OF HOMELAND SECURITY—a.k.a. DHS ORIGINS

The DHS has the shortest history of all of the intelligence organizations we will explore in this book. That's because it was virtually born yesterday.

Before the 9/11 destruction of the World Trade Center, law prevented the FBI and the CIA from operating effectively together to avert terrorism on US soil. The FBI was focused on criminal apprehension and prosecution, and the CIA was focused on intelligence gathering, counterintelligence, and counterterrorism abroad. The Bureau and the Company were not allowed to share most of their information with each other due to civil rights concerns.

This efficiency gap could have been closed at low cost to taxpayers with a bit of well-crafted legislation. However, Congress, never one to do for a dollar what it can do for thirty-eight billion dollars, created the DHS. Its intent in establishing the DHS was to set up an agency that could work with itself in order to prevent the next 9/11.

PURPOSE

The original core mission of the DHS was counterintelligence in order to ensure a homeland that is "safe and secure," whatever that means. In reality, we're not sure the DHS knows what it exists to do, and if it does know, it's neither denying nor confirming what that might be.

We aren't being as glib as we sound to say that. Congress, apparently unaware that America already had a Central Intelligence Agency to oversee other intelligence agencies, created what is in many ways a duplicate organization when it created the DHS. Since its initial creation, its main purpose seems to be justifying its existence by collecting other organizations under its food chain umbrella. Young and growing like the adolescent it is, the DHS is constantly being created by both internal ambitions and outside forces such as Congress and any given president. Since the inception of the DHS, the department has grown to include the Federal Emergency Management Agency, the Coast Guard, the Secret Service, Immigration and Customs Enforcement, Border Patrol, the Transportation Security Administration ("TSA"), and much more.

According to the DHS web site, its mission statement at the time of this publication is as follows:

"With honor and integrity, we will safeguard the American people, our homeland, and our values . . . Missions include preventing terrorism and enhancing security; managing our borders; administering immigration laws; securing cyberspace; and ensuring disaster resilience."

We are not certain if "our values" means the values of the American people, which are in no way cohesive, the values of the current administration, which are not representative of all Americans, the values of the DHS bureaucrats, which we don't know, or the values of writers in the PR department who came up with the mission statement. Only one thing is certain. Whatever the DHS mission is at this moment, it is not likely to remain the same.

JURISDICTION

DHS operates inside the United States everywhere from the Coast Guard patrolling American shores to the TSA agents patting down elderly Mennonite ladies at the airport to the undercover vans filled with vehicle-scanning equipment that patrol our streets and highways. Outside the United States, the DHS is supposed to work in cooperation with the CIA for its surveillance and apprehension endeavors; however, that boundary is a gray area that has never quite been defined.

SCOPE OF OPERATIONS

The DHS can order surveillance on anyone inside the United States for virtually any reason under the Patriot Act and its legal progeny. The TSA in our airports, our train stations, our bus stations, and on our highways and streets can scan or search anyone inside the United States at any time for virtually any reason, and it can collect and download the entire contents of any electronic devices of individuals entering the country, both American citizens and foreigners, when they enter from abroad. The various agencies and organizations under the auspices of the

DHS have virtually unlimited surveillance and apprehension power within the United States.

To spy on people outside of the United States, the DHS has its own personnel, but it also relies on the NSA, the CIA, and other agencies. This is a gray area with a great deal of overlap.

ARRESTING AUTHORITY

Like the FBI, the DHS is authorized to arrest people inside the United States. Also like the FBI, the DHS must obtain the cooperation of a foreign country to apprehend suspects in their territory. Also like the FBI, anyone arrested by the DHS inside American jurisdiction has all the rights they would have if they were arrested by any other US police body, such as the right to remain silent and the right to an attorney. In theory, anyone arrested inside American jurisdiction by the DHS should appear in the US legal system. We have no idea how strictly DHS does or does not comply with this official position.

If the DHS nabs someone overseas, that person will *likely* show up in the US judicial system. There are allegations that the DHS can detain people in places outside of the United States if it does not want those people in the US judicial system. President Bush was open about this. It has been alleged that these extra-judicial detainments also occurred under the Obama administration. Former president Obama prefers not to talk about such things. As for President Trump, if you ask him about it on Twitter, there's a good chance that he will give you a more colorful answer than we are at liberty to give.

OVERSIGHT

Unlike the CIA, the FBI, or the NSA, the DHS has full department status. That means it is a large departmental bucket that contains an ever-growing number of agencies. Its contents change depending on the agendas of Congress and the president at any given time.

In theory, the DHS is supposed to report to the Director of National Intelligence. In reality, it does so only nominally. Also in theory, the DHS is subject to congressional oversight. The DHS has its own departmental head, which is a cabinet position that reports directly to the president. Because the DHS is its own department, it has whatever power the president decides to give it on any given day.

In our opinion, there are undoubtedly many outstanding and dedicated employees at the DHS. We appreciate their dedication, and we have no criticism of them as individuals. If we sound biased against the DHS, it is because we object to the basic structure, management, and lack of oversight of the department, and we object to a secret police force having policing power over US citizens. We view such a combination of powers as fundamentally un-American.

Writing Tip: With its direct line to the president, combined with both surveillance authority and arresting authority, DHS is the intelligence and law enforcement body that has virtually unlimited secret police powers. Dystopian thriller writers can find a wealth of despotism in this arrangement. One excellent example of this entirely feasible use of Department of Homeland Security power is the TV series *Colony*.

NATIONAL SECURITY AGENCY/CENTRAL SECURITY SERVICE—a.k.a. NSA/CSS, NSA

We must begin this section with an admission—Bayard & Holmes have a bit of a biased impression of the NSA. However, we are committed to bringing you objective information in spite of our personal biases. Therefore, we have invited retired US Navy SEAL and NSA spook Rob DuBois, founder of Impact Actual*, to provide his perspective in an effort to balance our somewhat cynical view of the agency.

ORIGINS

Modern signals intelligence ("SIGINT") began with Herbert Osborn Yardley's Black Chamber Operation in the early twentieth century. Yardley was a railroad telegrapher from Worthington, Indiana. He was also a poker player, and he used his winnings to pay for classes at the University of Chicago. In 1912, he became a telegrapher for the US government and worked as a code clerk in the US State Department. While he was there, he amused himself by cracking American codes without using ciphers. He noticed President Wilson was using a ten-year-old code from previous presidents and was appalled. He promptly cracked the code without a cipher and without breaking a sweat. At that point, the United States began taking its codes more seriously.

War brewed on the horizon, and in 1917, Yardley joined the US Army and became a second lieutenant in the US Army Signal Corps. He established the Military Intelligence Section 8, or "MI8," and began the Black Chamber Operation for the purpose of studying the radio and telegraph traffic of the warring parties in Europe, paying particular attention to breaking German codes. The Black Chamber was located in an office in New York City and jointly funded by the US State Department and the US Army until it was shut down for budget reasons in 1929. Even after that, though, a skeleton crew still operated on the fringe.

In 1931, Herbert O. Yardley became the first "celebrity spook" by publishing his memoirs, *The American Black Chamber*. The book was a smash hit. It was translated into French, Swedish, Japanese, and Chinese and sold over fifty thousand copies. It's also estimated that Yardley's bestseller alerted nineteen countries to the fact that their codes had been broken.

The US government was not amused. Yardley had not violated any existing laws, so Congress amended the Espionage Act to prohibit disclosure of foreign code or of anything sent in code. Yardley's second book, *Japanese Diplomatic Codes: 1921-1922*, was seized by US marshals and kept classified until 1979.

The appearance of *The American Black Chamber* on the market created a public outcry at a time when espionage was considered to be uncivilized and reading someone else's mail to be barbaric. It was at that point that Secretary of State Henry L. Stimson realized the cryptanalysts of the Black Chamber Operation weren't just encrypting US communications, they were decrypting the codes of other nations. Stimson was outraged. "Gentlemen don't read other gentlemen's mail." It didn't help that Yardley bragged in a meeting with Stimson that he could read 100 percent of the Vatican's traffic any time he wanted. Stimson withdrew State Department support for the operation. Congress—the same Congress that had happily funded the Black Chamber Operation—strutted its outrage and demanded that the operation be completely shut down. (Refer to The Life Cycle of Controversial Practices mentioned in the CIA section.)

There are disagreements in historical records about the exact dates that the Black Chamber Operation was in process. That's in part because Yardley and the US Army wanted the details to be confusing as a way of protecting the operation from members of

Congress, the media, and the public that would be hostile to the idea of the United States reading other people's mail. This tactic of putting out conflicting or inaccurate information is common in clandestine operations. It is an important tool that helps keep operations covert.

The confusion around the historical records of the Black Chamber Operation is also due to the many different agendas that were simultaneously in play at the time. Then, just as today, congressmen and media were willing to say anything to further their own interests. Also then, just as today, various good and decent people genuinely believed inaccurate data, while the few who actually had firsthand knowledge said little or nothing at all.

Writing Tip: For increased accuracy in fiction, have your spooks deliberately disseminate inaccuracies to the public for the purpose of protecting their clandestine operations.

There is no telling if the US Army simply went "across the street" and continued business as usual on the day the Black Chamber Operation closed its doors in 1931. It's entirely possible. But what we do know for certain is that the US Army was training cryptanalysts again by the mid-1930s. It routinely graduated personnel from SIGINT schools long before Pearl Harbor, and those personnel were well trained in field and tactical communications and intercepts.

The US Navy also ran its own signals intelligence operations focusing on decrypting Japanese codes while the US Army focused on the Soviets and Europe. These operations were not entirely independent of one another, but overall, they operated separately. The Joint Chiefs of Staff were aware of these projects. However, no one mentioned them to Congress, the State Department, or the Justice Department. The US Army and the US Navy didn't want to get operations off the ground and running smoothly just to have Congress shut them down. As for President Franklin Roosevelt, it seems he was not too keen for any details.

That being said, some congressmen had to have known and been complicit. In the 1920s and 1930s, Congress picked over the US Army and US Navy budgets like vultures on a half-dry carcass. SIGINT schools were operating, which means they were being funded. It would appear that Congress was comfortable with those operations so long as it could pretend it didn't know about the operations.

In 1942, the US Army used the War Powers Act to take possession of Arlington Hall for use by its Signals Intelligence Service. However, evidence leads some historians to believe the US Army was paying for space to house its SIGINT operations in there long before its official acquisition. By 1943, the military could no longer keep the existence of its signals intelligence projects clandestine. With WWII in full swing, there was simply too much activity. Congress found out about the military SIGINT operations, along with the fact that the military had been developing the programs since the mid-1930s. The dam broke, and the Venona project was born.

The Venona project, a joint military and civilian operation that eventually came under the auspices of the NSA, officially ran from 1943 until 1980. During that time, it was crucial in decrypting Soviet transmissions. Among its most well-known successes were the rooting out of Julius and Ethel Rosenberg and Soviet espionage of the Manhattan Project, as well as Donald Maclean and Guy Burgess of the Cambridge Five spy ring. (See our upcoming release, *Key Figures in Espionage: The Good, the Bad, and the Booty*.)

By November 4, 1952, both Congress and the American public commonly recognized that the Soviet Union was a clear and present danger to the United States, and that the United States needed signals intelligence as a matter of national security. To that end, the US government established the National Security Agency/Central Security Service to perform SIGINT operations on behalf of the United States.

PURPOSE

The NSA's mission statement as stated on its web site at the time of publication is as follows:

"The National Security Agency/Central Security Service (NSA/CSS) leads the U.S. Government in cryptology that encompasses both Signals Intelligence (SIGINT) and Information Assurance (IA) products and services, and enables Computer Network Operations (CNO) in order to gain a decision advantage for the Nation and our allies under all circumstances."

Since that's a pretty meaningless collection of words, we'll clarify. Cryptology is the core of the NSA/CSS. The agency's job is to break foreign codes and set codes for the entire US government. As a part of that effort, the NSA employs linguists to analyze the content of communications and glean information about the people who construct the messages. The NSA also audits and ensures that safety protocols are being followed at government installations, and it listens to and stores foreign and domestic signals.

Technically, the NSA is supposed to share the information it gathers with the military and intelligence communities. In reality, the NSA has a well-earned reputation for being extremely stingy at sharing anything at all.

That being said, in the interests of objectivity ...

According to our SEAL/NSA adviser Rob, this near-paranoid protection of collection is due to extreme caution about revealing "sources and methods," those critical elements without which the NSA could not perform its vital national security mission. If information is exposed that could only have been acquired through one specific technical or procedural channel, that exposure can lead to a complete loss of visibility over serious threats. For example, once Osama bin Laden's use of his satellite telephone was identified in a national American paper, he quit using it, and the NSA lost that important source. It can take as little as one mention of the information or, as in the bin Laden instance, the source of the information, and that source is burned. As a result, the NSA protects its technical sources and methods as severely as the CIA protects its human and technical assets. It is a necessity that can leave those outside the NSA with the false impression that the agency is "extremely stingy."

Thank you, Rob.

We want to emphasize that the NSA is peopled with outstanding employees who provide responses to specific surveillance requests made by other military and civilian government organizations. However, the NSA as an agency, for whatever reason, is not given to sharing its information under any circumstances other than direct agency requests for surveillance, and it has developed a certain reputation within the military and intelligence communities for being tightfisted. In fact, military branches and intelligence organizations view the NSA as a black hole where information and money go in, and nothing comes out.

> "The NSA is undoubtedly the source of astronomers' models of cosmological black holes." ~ Jay Holmes

USS *LIBERTY* INCIDENT

One clear example of this non-sharing of information is the information the NSA has non-shared for decades about the USS *Liberty* incident. On June 8, 1967, during the Six-Day War between Israel and Egypt, Israeli aircraft and torpedo boats attacked the clearly marked US Navy signals intelligence ship, the USS *Liberty*, while she was underway in international waters off the coast of Sinai. That assault resulted in the deaths of 34 US Navy crewmen and the serious injury of 171-one more. (See *Key Moments in Espionage*.)

On that day, a US Navy signal intelligence team was flying a mission to monitor signals in that area. The team reports turning in at least four tapes to the US Navy at the end of their flight. Those four tapes were subsequently turned over to the NSA.

US Navy Admiral Isaac Kidd, a highly respected officer with an impeccable reputation, was tasked with investigating the attack on the USS *Liberty*. He and his staff specifically requested the four tapes that were turned over by the signal intelligence team. In response, the NSA coughed up only two of the recordings, and the information on them contained obvious time gaps. The NSA denied the existence of any other tapes. Admiral Kidd was quite blunt about saying his investigation was stymied from the start, and that there was a severe and obvious cover-up around the USS *Liberty* incident. Some members of the US Navy believe that the NSA still retains the rest of the tapes to this day.

Side Note: We again want to emphasize that the NSA has some excellent personnel, all traitorous private contractors hoarding information in their basements aside. We will be ecstatic if those excellent NSA personnel are ever allowed to do their jobs and actually share the information they collect with other government branches.

Conflict Alert: Have your characters, whether military, intelligence, Congress, or citizen, request collected information from the NSA. Delay NSA callbacks, e-mails, and responses of any kind. When your characters finally do get in touch with someone at the NSA, make sure that person is as obstructive as possible.

JURISDICTION

Most NSA employees reside and operate inside the United States, though they might travel to US embassies or foreign bases. Anywhere on the planet that the US government operates secured communications, the NSA has the authority to show up and investigate to make sure that security procedures are in place. The NSA neither confirms nor denies having any facilities of its own outside of the United States for the purpose of gathering signals.

Conflict Alert: If your characters working at government installations don't have enough turmoil and trauma, throw in an NSA audit. We wholeheartedly support the NSA in its efforts to make sure that security protocols are in place and being followed by government personnel. In fact, we hope they will decide to make a visit to the State Department in the very near future. However, any government, military, or civilian office can attest to the fact that an inspection of any kind by any agency, no matter how discreet, causes heightened tensions.

SCOPE OF OPERATIONS

The NSA does not discuss its foreign and domestic intelligence gathering operations. However, we would encourage you to allow your imaginations to run wild.

> **Writing Tip:** According to public sources, for the sake of authenticity, there is no need to hold back in your fiction when it comes to the extent and capabilities of government surveillance of citizens, noncitizens, people inside our borders, people living in foreign countries, people in dense urban areas, people on deserted islands, people inside their homes, people outside their homes, people on their phones, people on social media, people chatting at their neighbor's kitchen table, people at the International Space Station . . . You get the idea.

ARRESTING AUTHORITY

The NSA does not arrest anyone. Not ever.

We know what you're thinking . . . But wait! I saw that episode of *Numbers* where the NSA agents were in the field hunting down jihadis. . . .

Yes. We know the one. There are many such fictions in fiction. But we'll pick on the episode of *Numbers* where an NSA team shows up at FBI headquarters because they are hunting down a jihadi they picked up information on overseas . . . No . . . Just. No. And for the record, the NSA also does not kill people, fake killing people, or "disappear" people as on *Elementary*, either, though some of the spooks at the NSA might have wanted to after seeing those episodes in Season Two.

The NSA is in charge of doing audits at government sites. They come on-site, report to the code room, and see what they find there. Their purpose for the audit is to make sure everything is in compliance. They don't send out teams to local police departments or to the FBI to chase down jihadis.

Officially, if an NSA agent is in the field to investigate, detain, or do long-term surveillance on someone in the United States, they would have someone from FBI counterintelligence with them, and the NSA agent would be sitting in the backseat of the car. No one in the FBI is buying dinner for them. The NSA agent will pay their own way. If the NSA agent is abroad, it's the CIA they would ride along with, and it goes like this . . . "What? You want to go with us? You're buying dinner."

Unofficially, there have been claims, including the relatively recent allegations by Edward Snowden, that the NSA has overstepped its official charter and has conducted surreptitious entry for the purpose of physically bugging locations of targeted individuals overseas.

Bottom Line: If someone shows up at your home flashing an NSA badge and threatening to break down your door and arrest you, feel free to shoot them if the laws of your state allow you to legally defend yourself in that way. They are a Hollywood crew and not NSA employees. . . . At the very least mace them, throw colorful Shakespearean insults at them, and call 911.

OVERSIGHT

That's a good question. In fact, the question of NSA oversight has been afloat for many decades. Technically, the NSA is supposed to report to the national director of intelligence and to the CIA, but the CIA has never been satisfied with the NSA's sharing of information.

Everyone in the NSA leadership serves at the pleasure of the president. As with the CIA, the president likes to pretend that he forgot that the NSA does what he tells it to do. For example, Edward Snowden's little bombs resulted in a great deal of presidential and congressional amnesia. Refer to The Life Cycle of Controversial Practices mentioned previously in the CIA section and insert "NSA" instead. Except for Step Ten. We can neither confirm nor deny whether NSA employees hold barbecues or laugh. Our SEAL/NSA adviser Rob DuBois has hinted that these things may possibly, allegedly happen, but only if all the NSA operators/celebrants are safely locked into secure, windowless spaces.

---

*Impact Actual is a program devoted to helping people overcome obstacles and hardships to meet their life goals in the belief that the power to change the world comes through changing ourselves. Learn more about Rob DuBois and his programs at ImpactActual.com. Thank you, again, Rob, for your input. All the best to you and Impact Actual.

10

ELECTRONIC SURVEILLANCE

ENCYCLOPEDIAS CAN BE WRITTEN ON ELECTRONIC SURVEILLANCE, and between the time the authors start and finish, their work is obsolete. In fact, someone can write a pamphlet on the topic, and in the time that takes, the information is obsolete. Electronic surveillance is the fastest-growing area of espionage to date. It is not our field of expertise, and we won't even attempt to give you a comprehensive summary of electronic surveillance. What we will do, though, is hit some electronic-surveillance highlights to posit sound ideas about what's happening and what's possible.

For more detailed cybersecurity information, pick up *Cybersecurity for Executives: A Practical Guide*. It comes recommended by Chris Magill, an Information Security Professional and privacy advocate who helps companies manage their cryptographic systems and hunts down hackers. According to him, it is a concise, readable overview of information security.

GOVERNMENT SECTOR

At the inception of the Patriot Act during the Bush 2.0 administration, a substantial portion of the population was deeply concerned that the relaxing of the requirement for probable cause in any surveillance on American soil would lead to unbridled surveillance of American citizens. As the public found out when Edward Snowden dropped his media bombs, this was no unfounded concern.

According to public sources, modern technology allows for the interception and storage of every electronic transmission from phone calls, e-mails, and texts, to bank transactions, medical records, library card usage, etc. All of this is known as "raw data," and it is possible to store it indefinitely.

According to public sources, the NSA collects and stores all of this raw data. *According to public sources*, the Five Eyes Countries—the United States, United Kingdom, Canada, Australia, and New Zealand—along with Israel and possibly other countries have direct access to the raw data that they all collect and store on their own citizens and foreign nationals. *According to public sources*, the US government, through the NSA, has agreements for information exchange with corporations. All of this information became available in various public sources after Edward Snowden's info dump in 2013.

We know what you're thinking . . . Why all of the repetitive bold italic type in the previous paragraphs? . . . Because even Bayard & Holmes need to cover their asses at times.

The Obama administration's initial reaction to the Snowden Dump was denial. Then Obama switched to saying he knew about it and that it wasn't going to stop because it was helping prevent terrorism. Many in the public accepted Obama's assessment and applauded the president for having the courage to protect them from terrorists. However, many in the public resented the trampling of their civil rights and the expenditure of vast treasures of taxpayer cash to spy on Americans.

When more and more information was revealed about the US government's data collection programs, President Obama finally declared his outrage and promised that he would get that naughty NSA under control. In 2015, Congress passed the USA Freedom Act, which purports to limit NSA surveillance on Americans and end the bulk collection of data. (Refer to The Life Cycle of Controversial Practices mentioned previously in the CIA Section.)

In July of 2016, the Department of Justice, which, as you will remember, reports directly to the president, proposed legislation to Congress for cross-border data sharing. According to the American Civil Liberties Union, this data sharing would do the following:

- Allow foreign governments to acquire the content of stored communications of Americans and foreigners without a warrant.
- Allow foreign governments to request that US companies assist in real-time surveillance.
- Provide an end-run around the protections of the Fourth Amendment and Wiretap Act.
- Grant the executive branch broad discretion to enter into bilateral agreements that weaken privacy protections for Americans and foreigners.
- Weaken existing privacy protections by eliminating individualized review of information requests.
- Contain inadequate oversight to ensure that technology companies are only turning over information that is consistent with the terms of a particular agreement.
- Permit information disclosures that do not meet human-rights standards.

See 2016 Joint NGO Letter to Congress on Cross-Border Data Sharing, which can be found at https://www.hrw.org/news/2016/08/09/joint-ngo-letter-congress-cross-border-data-sharing, and US Cross-Border Data Deal Could Open Surveillance Floodgates, which can be found at https://www.hrw.org/news/2017/09/18/us-cross-border-data-deal-could-open-surveillance-floodgates.

In March of 2018, President Trump signed the Clarifying Lawful Overseas Use of Data (CLOUD) Act. This Act is cross-border data sharing legislation that allows the American government to compel companies to turn over the data they collect on their servers and in data centers overseas. The Act also allows the executive branch to make agreements with the governments of "select nations" that permit those governments to obtain data directly from US companies without any review by the US government. The concerns are the same concerns that are listed above.

For details, see Cross-Border Data Sharing Under the CLOUD Act at https://fas.org/sgp/crs/misc/R45173.pdf by legislative attorney Stephen P. Mulligan for Congressional Research Service.

Writing Tip: This universal electronic surveillance has grave consequences for any of your characters trying to go "off the grid." Because of this surveillance, the first and best choice is for characters to have a new identity and to hide in plain sight. If that isn't possible, they will need to use cash, their source of income needs to be cash, and they must pay their bills without using their real name because utility companies will sell their information or give it to the police. Characters in hiding need to stay off the Internet, avoid ATMs, avoid parking lot cameras, use disposable phones, take out phone batteries, use older vehicles without any Bluetooth or Internet capabilities, etc. They should also avoid interactive electronics of all kinds, including children's toys. They should not meet any friends with electronic devices on them, as well.

PRIVATE SECTOR

Yes, Virginia, corporations really can and do spy on their customers.

People are worried about the government taking their information and using it against them. However, they are all too often looking in the wrong place for trouble. Corporations are far more motivated to suck every byte of data about us from all available sources than most governments are, and they are more than happy to sell or trade that information to governments.

You may have noticed the following:

- You chat with a friend on Facebook about an item, and suddenly ads for that item start popping up everywhere you go in the cyberverse.
- You google an item, and ads for that item show up on other sites.
- You purchase an item with a credit card, and ads for that item start showing up on your Facebook page and in the margin of your e-mail.
- You mention an item in an e-mail, and ads appear during your browsing.
- You think you're having a private conversation in your own home about a product, and the product ad pops up later that same day on your computer.
- You talk about a product in the vicinity of your cell

phone, and ads for that product appear on your Facebook page.

This is not coincidence. Every electronic footprint you make is recorded in the place that you make it, and it is sold to other parties.

For example, Piper literally just took a call on her *landline* from an Edward Jones consultant as she was drafting this section at her computer. At no time did she say "Edward Jones" during the conversation. She hung up and immediately clicked on a YouTube link. An Edward Jones ad popped up. Creepy. As. Hell. It's because her landline provider and her Internet provider are the same company.

Bottom Line: It's not just the government; Google, Facebook, Twitter, etc., are also spying on us. Our phone companies are spying on us all for their own profits, as well.

Social media sites also communicate with our credit card companies. For example, Piper heard about Bragg's Organic Apple Cider Vinegar from a friend, and she purchased a bottle with her credit card. The next day, an ad for Bragg's Organic Apple Cider Vinegar popped up in the margin of her Facebook page.

We know what you're thinking . . . Wait! What? How could Bragg's know to target Piper from her credit card purchase, and how did it legally make its way to her Facebook page?

Credit card corporations have vague privacy practices that allow them to sell information on what we purchase to other corporations. For example, Piper's credit card agreement states that her card company can share information on her transactions and experiences, and that it can enter into joint marketing with other financial companies. Facebook is a "free" site worth billions. Facebook has to get that billionaire status from somewhere, and what richer fields could be plowed for targeted ads?

In fact, speaking of Facebook, as this book is in the publishing process, Facebook founder Mark Zuckerberg is having to answer some uncomfortable questions about Facebook's data collection, which even extends to people who do not have Facebook accounts. Squirm, Mark. Squirm.

> *"If you're not paying for it, you're not the customer; you are the product being sold."* ~ Andrew Lewis, a.k.a. blue_beetle

Corporations pay big money to focus their advertising efforts throughout the Internet. A little agreement between a corporation, a credit card company, and Facebook, and, voilà, an ad going to a known consumer. The chain from Piper's credit card purchase to the Facebook ad on her page just got shorter. Sure, it could have been coincidence that a product Piper had only just heard of and bought once should so quickly appear at the side of her profile page, and it could also be coincidence that water always flows downhill.

Fasten your seat belts. This has not yet begun to get creepy.

We all remember *1984* by George Orwell, in which Big Brother watches people inside their homes through their television sets. You know those "smart" TVs, those computers with cameras and mics, those refrigerators, dishwashers, and microwaves that connect to the Internet . . . the phones, iPads, Fitbits, and children's toys with cameras, mics, and Internet capabilities? If it has a camera and it hooks to the Internet, it can watch you. If you can speak to the device and it links to the Internet, it can listen to you. Corporations even collect data on sexual activity from net-centric vibrators. Which begs the question ... who would care to do that? ... Just. Ew.

The obvious answer is the US government. That's old news. Although the NSA is going for its own *Hoarders: Digital Edition* prime-time slot, most American administrations so far would only use the power of the NSA to spy on Americans in efforts to contain terrorist activities.

What most people don't realize is that *foreign* governments and corporations can and do spy on Americans. Think about it. If corporations are already harvesting information on your grocery purchases, your Google searches, your Facebook activities, etc., why wouldn't they also use every other tool at their disposal, up to and including the cameras and mics that you, yourself, bring into your house? They can and do.

"This is especially true if it is an item made in China, or if it is an item that is made in a country that shares the same planet with China." ~ Jay Holmes

---

Almost all electronic components of every computer or television of every brand are made in Asia. You know. That place where China hangs out. China is an aggressive country with the world's largest economy, and it harbors dreams of world domination. China, Russia, and corporations spy on average individuals as a matter of course.

The spyware doesn't just come packaged in the electronics. People daily invite it into their computers and other electronics with apps. You know that innocent little pop-up in which a company—often the maker of the electronic device—asks if you will permit it to make changes to your computer? The correct answer is always NO. In fact, a more accurate answer would be, "Oh, *hell* no, you filthy rat-bastards. I'd sooner sell my mother to a Tel Aviv brothel."

And what about those good friends Siri and Alexa and their kin, who are always so quiet until you ask them to do your bidding? Think of them as entire teams of marketing specialists and hostile government spies sitting in your living room.

We know. The same question occurs to most people . . . Why would they do that? I'm just not that interesting.

The first answer is that China gonna China. China routinely collects all of the information it can on everyone. In one confirmed case, Chinese-based company Shanghai AdUps Technology installed a "back door" on over seven hundred million Android phones, which sends text messages, call log, contact list, location history, and app data to servers in China every seventy-two hours. The AdUps software is also capable of remotely installing and updating applications on the Androids. Whether the data is being collected for advertising purposes or government surveillance or both is anybody's guess. The consumer can neither opt out nor disable the technology.

Foreign governments have any number of reasons for spying on foreign nationals that most Americans, even novelists, can't imagine. For example, China makes a regular practice of hunting down its expatriates in the West. The program is known as Operation Fox Hunt. (See <u>Bayard & Holmes Operation Fox Hunt—China Targets Its Expatriates</u> at http://bayardandholmes.com/2015/08/17/operation-fox-hunt-china-targets-its-expatriates/.) Also, Iran has at least three intelligence agencies devoted to spying on its own expatriates. Those agencies are like middle school girls trying to dig up dirt on each other and everyone around them. They would LOVE electronic access into people's homes just to have something to talk about on the way to the mosque.

These are only a few reasons foreign governments want to spy on *you*:

- To spy on expatriates
- To monitor trends in society
- To improve training of deep-cover operatives
- To better design propaganda efforts in foreign countries
- To gather information on possible targets for covert action
- To identify blackmail targets
- To build files on important foreigners

And, of course, money is a fantastic motivator for both governments and private corporations in the information chain. Information translates into targeted marketing, which then translates into money. Corporations have agreements with other corporations and with server hosts that can perform all manner of word recognition. Computers automatically scan, transmit, and respond.

But how can Western corporations legally do this with products sold in America and the rest of the West?

Let's take a look at some of the contract language that people agree to when they use these items. Keep in mind as you read this that computers are legally even easier to use for corporate and foreign government espionage than they are for American government espionage.

In February of 2015, one Smart TV online manual included the following clause regarding its voice recognition technology:

"Please be aware that if your spoken words include personal or other sensitive information, that information will be among the data captured and transmitted to a third party through your use of Voice Recognition."

In other words, anything you say in range of the microphone will be captured and transmitted to a third party. We'll get back to that "third party" bit in a moment.

It was brave and honest language regarding the voice recognition process. The public noticed this language, and many people objected. The company responded by changing its written description, but not its product.

[Redacted Company Name]'s later online manual read as follows:

"... the voice data consists of TV commands, or search sentences, only...."

And...

"[Redacted Company Name] does not sell voice data to third parties."

On the surface, this language sounds reassuring. Let's see what this language is and is not saying.

In the first paragraph...

"... the voice data consists of TV commands, or search sentences, only." That doesn't mean that the only thing the TV hears is specific commands or specific search sentences. It means the TV is transmitting all conversations in range of the mic to a third party vendor, which sorts through what is said to detect anything defined as "voice data" to determine if anyone is giving a command to the TV. Also, "search sentences" could mean pretty much anything. It could mean "Turn on TV," or it could mean

"Bragg's Organic Vinegar," or it could mean "I'll be flying to Singapore this weekend."

Generally, if people are talking normally in a room with a mic, the mic will activate and scan the conversation for any voice commands. So, basically, any time people are talking over a whisper in a room with a Smart TV, they are conducting a search as far as the TV is concerned.

The first sentence of the second paragraph states, "[Redacted Company Name] does not sell voice data to third parties." According to the company's own definition of "voice data," the words which constitute voice data are only a tiny percentage of what the TV's mic transmits. There is no statement regarding what else the company might sell of what is collected and transmitted to the third party vendor. There is also no statement regarding what the third party vendor might sell.

But the TV and [Redacted Company Name] are not, themselves, necessarily the primary spies in the room. What about all of the apps? Here's what [Redacted Company Name] has to say about that:

"The third-party apps . . . are controlled by third parties and therefore they have their own set of terms and conditions."

In other words, even when the TV itself isn't listening and transmitting your conversations to third party vendors, your apps could be spying on you through the TV.

And what does [Redacted Company Name] have to say about that all-important third party vendor?

"[Redacted Company Name] does not release information about our third-party vendors."

That could be a blank check. The third party vendors could be foreign governments, private corporations, or individuals, and they could be collecting, trading, selling, storing, etc., all of your conversations picked up by the mic.

Smart TV manuals from other companies vary in their disclosure. One says right up front that they are collecting "household demographic data" and sharing it with other companies. Another makes it a point to reassure its customers that the "TV" is not recording their conversations without explaining that the TV is a transmitter, not a recorder. And still another company manual doesn't address the topic at all.

To be clear, we are *not* accusing any specific electronics company of anything illegal. This is *not* an indictment of [Redacted Company Name] or any other company.

We are using quotes from online manuals as random representative industry examples of the language, and we are noting the possibilities potentially legally afforded by the language. Using this sample language for the purpose of illustrating legal possibilities is in no way meant to imply that [Redacted Company Name] or any other company is breaking faith with its customers or doing any of the things we suggest are possible. In fact, Piper is rather fond of [Redacted Company Name]'s products and she uses them herself—just not the ones with Internet capabilities.

To be clear, nothing in this chapter or this book should be interpreted as legal advice.

If you believe you have a legal issue with your government, foreign governments, or corporations using your electronics to spy on you, please see a licensed attorney in your state.

Bottom Line: Electronics are constantly being updated to provide more conveniences for customers. Electronics manuals are constantly being updated, often sounding quite simple as they become more obtuse. It's important to remember there is always a dark side to the conveniences that we purchase, particularly when those conveniences are purchased with our privacy.

But take heart. We have good news. The Chinese aren't really very good at sifting, managing, and analyzing the data they collect. First, they don't have the technology to efficiently sort through all of that data. And second, they are hamstrung by groupthink and a profound need on an individual level to avoid getting into trouble. The Russians have vastly better technology to sift through their collected info, and they are not as hamstrung by groupthink and avoiding trouble as they have been in the past.

In other words, neither China nor Russia has any FBI Special Agent Penelope Garcia off of *Criminal Minds*.

Criminal Minds **Example:**

Prentiss: "Garcia, give me a list of all of the men who graduated from New York City high schools in 1978 that buy red running shoes from Walmart in June every year. Cross-reference that with anyone who ever said on social media that they love Labrador puppies."

Garcia: *three seconds later* "Got it! I've narrowed it down to fifteen."

Yeah, no. There is no "Penelope Garcia" or her magic computer in any government outside of Hollywood. Not in China. Not in Russia. Not even in the US . . . yet. In fact, if you find Penelope and her magic computer anywhere outside of Hollywood, please have her contact the NSA and the FBI. Our government needs her. In the meantime, China and Russia aren't going to be able to sift through our data like that.

PHONES

Phones are especially convenient for governments and corporations to use against people. They can use phones to locate and track people, collect conversations on and around the phone, and watch people through the phone cameras. Software can be embedded in phones by apps or at public WiFi locations. Phones also send signals that talk to other electronic devices around us.

Phone conversations are regularly intercepted by such things as the IMSI-catchers, or "stingrays," that police use to hijack cell phone connections to spy on people. Stingrays mimic wireless cell towers and "force" all surrounding cell phones and mobile devices to connect to it. Their use is widespread across America. It's an easy bet that DHS has perfected the art. The legality of such unwarranted police surveillance practices is still being debated in the courts.

Writing Tip: Reality places no boundaries on the vivid imagination where electronic surveillance is concerned.

Pro Tip: If a spook is overseas, they will assume that the resident government can and will intercept their phone conversations. The spook can use a small, encrypted satellite communications device to minimize what the opponent government collects. The government will still intercept the signal, but it will only receive electronic noise.

CAMERAS

When outside of your own house, assume cameras of every size are everywhere. Cameras can even be embedded in contact lenses. Samsung just patented the "smart contact" in 2016, and Google owns two patents for similar devices. They are controlled by blinking and can not only record and transmit what the wearer observes, but they can project images across the wearer's field of vision. And that is all we will say about that.

Writing Tip: No holds barred here. Run with it.

HACKERS

"There are only two kinds of Internet-connected devices—those that have been hacked and those that will be hacked." ~ Piper Bayard

---

Even the Pentagon gets hacked. If it's online, it's not 100 percent secure. Period. And hackers don't even have to pretend to follow laws or regulations. They can hack into phones, computers, TVs, vehicles, airplanes, kitchen appliances, and absolutely anything else that connects to the Internet.

To a certain extent, we can control our personal information at home in that we don't *have* to be on social media, we don't *have* to do our banking and bill paying online, and we don't *have* to reveal personal details of our lives in e-mail. But none of us can control what happens to our medical records, our credit card records, our children's school records, our banking records, or any other information that is in someone else's keeping.

Why would anyone want that information? Any number of reasons—identity theft, extortion, and blackmail, not to mention medical insurance identity theft. Medical insurance identity theft is one of the fastest-growing areas of crime. Thieves use the information for themselves, or they can sell it in bulk to others.

Foreign governments have an interest in hacking our information, as well. One of the most successful hacks in history was the Chinese hack of the US Office of Personnel Management in 2015. China gleaned hundreds of thousands of personnel files of US government workers, including intelligence personnel. The Chinese now have everything they need to winnow out US personnel in sensitive positions, personnel with medical issues, or personnel with weaknesses that can be extorted. Think of it as targeted marketing for espionage.

Bottom Line: When it comes to hacking, no computer or system is impenetrable if it connects to the Web, and no motive is too dastardly.

For more information on hacking, Information Security Professional Chris Magill recommends the Hacker Exposed series, which he says "is easy to understand and conversational despite its phone book-like dimensions. . . . It starts from an attacker's view and demystifies hacking."

For the basics of hacking in something smaller than a phone book, Information Security Professional Judy Towers recommends *The Basics of Hacking and Penetration Testing, Second Edition: Ethical Hacking and Penetration Testing Made Easy.*

We also recommend you follow Judy Towers on Twitter at @LadyRed_6 to stay current on cybersecurity issues.

Thank you, Chris and Judy!

CHILDREN'S TOYS

We would issue a special caution about interactive children's toys. Hackers can easily hack into your child's interactive Barbie, computer, special nightlight, whatever. If it talks to the Internet, it is vulnerable to hacking, and your child could be a target. For the safety of your children, we recommend that you NEVER bring net-centric children's toys into your home.

OUR CYBERSECURITY RECOMMENDATIONS:

- Don't bring a Smart TV or any other "smart" device into your home.
- If you do bring these things into your home, don't fool yourself into thinking the camera or mic is actually disabled just because you "turn it off."
- Cover all computer and other cameras in your house.
- Turn off your WiFi if you're talking on your phone near your computer.
- Use a dumb phone rather than a smart phone.
- If you must use a smart phone, do not use the Internet on your telephone.
- Do not download apps onto your telephone.
- Keep your phone in a Faraday Bag when you are out to avoid being tracked, or better yet, leave it at home.
- Turn off your phone's WiFi whenever you leave your home.
- Turn off your home's WiFi router whenever you leave.
- Do not pay your bills or do your banking online.
- Do not pay your taxes online.
- Change your passwords frequently on all of your accounts.
- Make your passwords truly random.

- Keep up-to-date security software on your computer.
- Limit any apps you download onto your computer.
- Don't go to questionable web sites.
- *Never* bring net-centric children's toys into your home. *Never*.
- Don't open e-mails from strangers.

What? ... Who lives like that?

We do. So do many government employees who know the power of electronic surveillance. Many don't even have Internet in their homes. Many would never go on social media. The fact is that you can't hack a piece of paper. Just ask our Bayard & Holmes attorney. He does everything on paper. We never worry about him getting hacked.

Bottom Line: If it is online, it is not secure. Period. Governments—ours and anyone else's—don't need to collect our data. They only need to ask corporations, the local library, the electric company, etc., for the information we freely give.

Writing Tip: When it comes to keeping electronic surveillance real in fiction, the sky is the limit. Pull out all the stops. If some of these creepy surveillance details don't have the plots raging through your head right now, you might want to consider taking up plumbing.

11

PHYSICAL SURVEILLANCE

THE DIGITAL AGE HAS FUNDAMENTALLY CHANGED SURVEILLANCE IN that now, most information is gleaned comparatively economically from electronics rather than from physically following a subject. Physical surveillance, as in actually keeping human eyes on a subject, is more expensive than digital surveillance both in human resources and financial resources. However, physical surveillance still has an indispensable place in espionage.

Before any physical surveillance occurs, a subject must be identified. Often this happens in conjunction with a crime or a tip. Sometimes identification is the product of ongoing investigations. Organized crime has deep roots, and evidence and information accumulate over time to point to suspects. Often, suspects are identified through the NSA's blanket electronic data mining of phone calls, social media, and financial transactions. For example, the NSA might notice that Grandma Habib calls Syria every week and investigate to see whether she is checking on her grandchildren or plotting a terrorist attack. The NSA might also pick up on financial transactions with Iraq and find out if Achmed is sending money to an orphanage or to a radical

Jihadicult. However a suspect is identified, one thing is certain. There must actually be a suspect for physical surveillance to occur. No organization, except possibly the DHS, has enough money and personnel to just hang out watching people and waiting for a crime to occur.

Once a subject is identified, the investigating body will monitor the subject's activity through cell phone, e-mail, credit card, banking transactions, and computers at work or at home. If something is picked up from intercepted electronic transmissions that indicates a specific event will occur at a specific time, such as an exchange of cash or information, the spooks or agents will place the subject under physical surveillance.

The first step to physical surveillance, whether domestic or international, is deciding where and when to start following the subject. This will be easiest if the spooks know where the subject lives or what hotel they are staying in, where they work, their favorite locations, and their associates. If the subject is in the United States, the FBI, DHS, or other agencies usually already know these things, or they will easily find them out. If international, it could take some digging, but that's something the CIA is good at.

DOMESTIC SURVEILLANCE

How surveillance is conducted by state and local law enforcement agencies and whether or not they function within legal parameters is outside our scope of knowledge. However, federal domestic surveillance is usually conducted by FBI, DHS, or another federal law enforcement agency, or it is conducted electronically by the NSA. Federal agencies and intelligence organizations contact the NSA and ask them to tag someone electronically for a specific job. In those instances, the NSA is excellent at actually turning over the information. This is an exception to the NSA Black Hole Rule discussed earlier.

With a domestic subject where an event is anticipated, an arrest is usually the objective of physical surveillance. In the case of FBI surveillance of a target, the Bureau will have a fair amount of personnel available, and they will try to listen to and record the conversation. They will be prepared to make an arrest if an exchange of cash or information takes place.

However, if no exchange occurs, the FBI might not make an arrest at that time. That's because once they make an arrest, the subject and their associates will become aware of the FBI investigation. That will make the subject and their associates much harder to catch at a later date. That's why it's important in FBI operations to be reasonably certain of prosecution before any arrests are made.

We can't say often enough that the FBI's purpose is prosecution in courts of law. Because of this, the FBI must have a genuine warrant to surveille a subject. A genuine warrant that will stand up in a court of law for the purposes of prosecution requires an actual named subject, probable cause, and a judge's blessing. The blanket FISA warrants that cause so much amnesia on Capitol Hill aren't good enough for FBI prosecution purposes.

The DHS has a broader surveillance mandate and can legally surveille multiple people in the process of getting to a single subject, so not all of its surveillance is for the purpose of prosecution. Or at least that is the impression they give everyone else in the IC. In truth, the DHS is fairly cagey about letting anyone know exactly what it does.

Bottom Line: The FBI is meticulous about following laws and rules when it comes to surveillance in order to make certain all of the evidence they gather is admissible in court. Not so much with the DHS.

Writing Tip: Pretty much anything an author writes about the DHS and domestic surveillance is plausible.

INTERNATIONAL SURVEILLANCE

When the CIA or other US intelligence organization conducts surveillance outside of the United States, how they do it depends largely on where they are conducting the surveillance. Surveillance in allied countries would involve the cooperation of those countries. Surveillance in not-so-allied countries might involve the cooperation of those countries, and it might not. And, of course, surveillance in hostile nations is a dangerous business.

If the United States wants a subject surveilled inside the United Kingdom, the US State Department or a CIA liaison might speak to the British government to obtain permission or to convince the British to conduct the surveillance and share the results. Alternatively, the CIA's liaison to MI5 or MI6 would communicate with MI5 or MI6, and if MI5 agrees, then MI5 would conduct the surveillance inside the United Kingdom. Technically, in theory, MI6 would not be directly involved in the surveillance, but sometimes what should occur and what does occur in reality are not always completely the same thing. Moving right along...

The rules and process would be similar with other close US allies with adequate surveillance resources and budgets, such as Canada or Australia. New Zealand, on the other hand, has a low budget for such things, so if the surveillance target were in New Zealand, the New Zealand government would call the United Kingdom, Australia, Canada, or even the United States and ask what they know about the person.

If the country is not a close ally but also not an enemy, such as a South American country, a decision would have to be made about whether or not to approach that country's government. That decision would depend on the United States' current relations with the foreign country.

Countries that receive foreign aid from the United States are often willing to cooperate temporarily in the surveillance of suspects inside their borders, though neither the State Department nor the US intelligence agencies would expect any real operational security during the process. In other words, if the situation warrants getting the country involved, the United States must assume that the subject will soon be notified that they are under surveillance by the foreign country's government, by our government, or by some combination thereof. *If* the United States chooses to not involve that country diplomatically, surveillance must be conducted secretly and without attracting any attention from the local government or other criminal organizations. That surveillance would be conducted primarily by the CIA.

Surveillance on subjects inside countries that are hostile to the United States would be conducted with the utmost secrecy. That surveillance would also be conducted primarily by the CIA.

So what does this look like in practice?

Let's say someone at the CIA identifies Schmucky Putavich in Bananastan as a person of interest. That person would recommend to the deputy director of the CIA that the CIA should watch Schmucky. The deputy director would say something like, "Yeah. Schmucky looks like he's up to something bad for us," and authorize the surveillance.

The investigating party at the CIA would then ask the NSA what it has on Schmucky. Such foreign surveillance was the NSA's original purpose, and it already has assets and procedures in place. The NSA would just need to pick that particular Schmucky insect out of the haystack, which it is excellent at doing. It could take the NSA a couple of hours or a few days to get back to the person asking.

While the NSA is looking under its rocks, the spook in charge of the operation might talk to the CIA chief of station in Bananastan to let the chief know that they want to watch Schmucky Putavich. The chief of station might or might not know something about Schmucky already, and the chief will give any feedback they have.

Then a team is picked out and sent to Bananastan. This could take between one day and one week, but rarely longer than a week.

Once the team is put together, a decision is made as to who's in charge. When the team arrives in Bananastan, they may or may not report to the chief of station. Sometimes they are the chief of station's responsibility, in which case they do report to the chief and involve the chief in their decisions. Once in country, the team decides when and where to conduct physical surveillance on Schmucky.

It's worth noting that in theory, the chief of station is considered the president's representative and is supposed to be kept apprised of all ongoing activities in their area of responsibility. In reality, if the deputy director deems it necessary to keep the team's presence under wraps, the team might not involve the chief of station at all. Chiefs of station are quite reasonably not big fans of things happening in their areas of responsibility without their knowledge, but sometimes things have to happen that way in the interests of security.

TRAILING TECHNIQUES

Once a surveillance team has picked the NSA's brain and assembled at a location in proximity to the target, the next step is to make a plan. They have to know what assets they have, how many man hours they want to use, and how many man hours are available in the budget. Everything has to be funded. The higher the priority of the targeted subject, the more man hours the government is willing to finance, so the importance of the subject will be the first factor in any surveillance plan. That plan can include people, vehicles, helicopters, drones, satellites, etc., and if the target is high priority, the team can expect more of those resources to be available.

Once a plan is in place, the team decides when and where to start the surveillance. Keep in mind that the surveillance will most likely be in anticipation of a particular transaction. If the subject's home address and work location are known, spooks can set up the surveillance ahead of time to follow the subject on a particular day. If the team is expecting the event to occur on a specific day, such as a Wednesday at noon, they can follow the target to work and to lunch. The team will try to observe and record whatever transaction it is they are expecting.

If the team is going to start on a weekday morning, they would have a vehicle in place, ready to follow that subject to work. The team would likely know the route and types of transportation the target takes to get to work. They would station a car at least two or three house lots away. Everywhere outside of Hollywood, real people notice total strangers staring at them from vehicles at the end of their driveway, their neighbor's driveway, or across the street. After all, don't *you* notice total strangers sitting in a car against the curb in front of your own house or your neighbor's? So do other people. And people who have a reason to be surveilled tend to be more paranoid than regular folk.

The spook in the vehicle would not make eye contact with the target or look in the target's direction when the target pulls out of his driveway. The spook would wait on the opposite side of the street until the target drove at least two hundred feet up the street. Then the spook would pull out from the curb. If the target is expected to head north, the spooks park *south* of his house. In Hollywood spooks are almost always parked the wrong direction. In real life, the spook doesn't let the target drive past him before pulling away from the curb. Too easy to be spotted.

If the team knows the route Schmucky Putavich will be taking, they will have multiple cars ready and waiting along that route, and they will pass him off at turns. If Schmucky does not have a regular route, the team will have several cars behind him. When Schmucky turns, the car at the front of the line will continue on straight, and the car that is second in line moves up to first and follows around the turn. The spook in what started out as the first car comes around and gets at the back of the line. This technique is best with four or more vehicles. Doing it with less than three is a bad idea.

If the team is afraid of losing Schmucky with physical surveillance, a spook will slip into Schmucky's garage or walk up to his car in the driveway at 3:00 a.m. and put a transponder on his vehicle. The transponder wouldn't be constantly active. It might have a low energy receiver that the team could use to turn it on, or it might have a motion detector that only transmits when the vehicle is in motion. The advantage to having the transmissions linked to motion is that it keeps the battery from running down as fast as it would if the transponder were transmitting signals 24/7. The transponder also can be set to continue transmitting for at least two minutes after the vehicle stops so it does not turn off at a traffic light.

Following someone on foot involves the same principles. A lone spook can't just be leaning against the target's front door in Manhattan and start following them the minute they walk outside. They would be so easy to spot that they might as well be wearing the "I'm a Spy" T-shirt. To effectively follow someone on foot, a spook must start from a distance and bring the team.

Again, if the route is known, people can be stationed to take over along the way. If it is not known, the team will work in the same way as a line of vehicles, with the person in front peeling off and coming around to the back of the line, either at a turn or at another juncture.

The team will likely ditch their electronics and communicate with physical signals because even headsets and earpieces are often too obvious. A signal might be taking off a hat or ducking into a café to indicate that the person behind should move up and take over. The last person in the line can also jump into a car and go ahead of the others if need be.

Another important reason to have more than one person for surveillance is that a spook might accidentally attract the notice of the target's security team. One of the first things spooks must learn about following people is not to be followed themselves. Smart targets with adequate resources will have a security team behind them watching out for anyone tailing them. That means that spooks can't only focus on who's in front of them. They have to be acutely aware of who is behind them, too. Otherwise, a target's henchmen will either put a bullet in the spook's head, snatch the spook off the street, or at a minimum alert the target that they are being followed.

We know what you're thinking . . . In Hollywood, all a spook has to do to follow a target on the street is duck into a doorway and peek around the corner. Why wouldn't a real spook just do that?

If a spook absolutely must follow a target on their own, and they need to watch said target from the cover of a doorway, stopping in a doorway to observe puts the "dead" into "dead giveaway." To avoid that dead factor, a spook must take their eyes off the target, go all the way inside a building, and only turn around once they are out of sight of the street. At that point, they can come back out and stop in the doorway under some other pretense than watching someone.

Imagine for a moment what it might be like when you've worked weeks, or even months or years, for a glimpse of Osama Jihadimaggot, and suddenly he's there in front of you, walking down the street. Finally, all of that Third World dysentery you've suffered while hunting down the bastard is paying off. Your hands are practically around his neck, preventing his next thousand victims. You've alerted your team, and you're tracking him back to his lair while they join you. You're keeping up, and there's no sign he's noticed you, but then he stops in the street to check out a vendor's melons. You have to find a way to stop, too, but that requires taking your eyes off of him to go all the way into a shop. He could be gone by the time you take that safety precaution. Maybe just this once . . .

That's what it's like for the spook in the field. It's sheer agony for them to take their eyes off of the target for that instant, and more than one spook has succumbed to the urge to cut corners "just this once." And more than one spook has died because of it.

But there is an upside to all of this caution about trailing henchmen—besides the obvious of not getting killed, of course. It gives spooks a chance to "clean up" any following entourage behind the target if they choose to do so. That would involve avoiding them, popping them off, or snatching them up, depending on the circumstances.

If a spook or team is following a suspect for the purpose of taking them down, they must be ready and willing to get into a gunfight. One example of this would be the arrest of Soviet spy and former US Naval Communications Technician John Walker, discussed above in the FBI chapter. Although the FBI had conducted a thorough and cautious surveillance and approach, at the time of his arrest, Walker was alert enough to draw a loaded handgun on the FBI agents. In that fraction of a second, the agents managed to convince Walker to drop his weapon.

From the Bayard & Holmes point of view, it's unfortunate that one of the FBI agents didn't accidentally shoot Walker in the groin, but the modern FBI is usually very careful to obey all laws and not make such moves. However, that incident should remind us that those being followed are often alert to the possibility that they are being surveilled.

Pro Tip: When peeking around walls and doors to keep their eyes on a subject or to check an area, a smart spook will squat down rather than stick their head out at head level. Head level is where a shooter will be looking.

Bottom Line: Professional physical surveillance requires a team wherever possible, not just a lone spook. If a lone spook, they must be exceedingly cautious, and they will likely lose the subject or be spotted.

Writing Tip: Trailing henchmen can provide excellent complications for spook characters and opportunities for realistic conflict and tension.

12

BUGGING SPACES

In spy parlance and crime stories, the term "bug" refers to electronic devices for clandestinely monitoring targeted spaces. We've all seen and read about fictional spooks locating bugs in homes, offices, and hotel rooms. The characters usually find them in a few seconds on lamp shades, behind pictures, and inside desk phones. And one of Piper's personal favorites, in the first season of *Homeland,* a CIA operative has illegally wired a military veteran's home, and she worries that someone will move the couch and see the bug. It's cute and convenient, but it's far from the truth.

After the Soviets successfully bugged the US ambassador's residential office in the US Embassy in Moscow from 1945–1952 with a gift of a carving of the US Great Seal, the US Central Intelligence Agency invested heavily in developing better bugging and bug-detection technology. The Company developed "audio teams," whose specialty it was to bug targeted spaces. Now, all modern intelligence services around the world field such specialty teams, and they are still called "audio teams" even though technology has since expanded into video capabilities.

Bugging technology has improved tremendously since audio teams were first formed, but it still uses some of the basic practices and principles developed prior to 1960. While other types of intelligence operatives partake in bugging activities as opportunities allow, when time and opportunity permit, a specialized team can do a better and less detectible installation.

We know what you're thinking . . . Why even bother to wire spaces when we have such efficient remote electronic surveillance?

Several reasons. First, electronic surveillance has the downside of being dependent on functioning equipment and systems, and equipment and systems don't always function properly. Second, some people are savvy enough to hold meaningful communications away from any of that equipment and systems, or to at least turn off any nearby electronics when they are conspiring. And third, physical bugs in a room are more reliable for collecting the information needed. Rather than hope the target places their electronics in helpful positions, spooks can place the equipment themselves to cover entire rooms and not just particular angles.

> **Bottom Line:** At the end of the day, nothing yet replaces good old-fashioned bugs.

Unscrupulous parties outside of government entities also still find physical bugging useful. Say a Mafia or a political party—if you still entertain a distinction between the two—want the inside scoop on a political candidate. It can be done one of two ways. A political leader owned by a party or a Mafia can manufacture an excuse to order surveillance. However, that might be rejected. Also, that political leader would be risking leaks to the intended target. The other way the dastardly villain can accomplish their goals surreptitiously is with physical bugging outside of government channels. Let's just say that a successful Watergate operation would be just as useful to political parties today as it would have been for Nixon in the seventies.

One downside of physical bugs is that a spook must actually access the space or intercept an item going to the space in order to plant the bug. Also, there is always the risk of the bug being discovered, which can lead to the target destroying it, reverse engineering it, or using it to feed the spook misinformation. Then there is the issue of power access. If a bug is in place without power access, it must be serviced regularly to keep it functioning.

WIRING A SPACE

How a space is wired and who does it depends on several factors, many of which can be summarized in one word—time.

1. How soon is the information needed?

If critical information is needed quickly, there may not be time for an audio team to show up and do a thorough job. In that case, one or more field operatives would wire the space. All field operatives have varying degrees of training and expertise in basic bugging techniques, and they usually have access to basic bugging equipment as part of their gear. We'll talk more about that below.

2. How long will the operative or audio team have access to set the bugs?

If a team or an operative only has a few minutes, then they will use the simplest installations of disguised bugs. If a specialty team has as much as twenty minutes to work, they consider it a luxury. Less time means a less thorough job, but in the field, operatives can't always control the time allotted for the task and must make do.

3. How sophisticated is the target?

The more sophisticated a target is, the more time an operative or an audio team will need to efficiently bug the space. With a less sophisticated target, such as a drug lord's lair or a Third World military or diplomatic installation, a good team can do a great job in as little as five minutes. With a more sophisticated target, such as a Russian embassy or a Communist China embassy, a six-man team can install a high-quality eavesdropping system in twenty minutes that would be extremely difficult for our enemies to detect.

4. How long must the power source for the bug last?

Transmitters, a.k.a. bugs, need a power source. This is always an issue. Bugs and cameras are now minute, and in the smallest devices, battery power is limited. However, technology does allow for bugs to use external power sources, such as the target's own electrical system. Bugs that draw power from the target's electrical system are optimal, as they can serve indefinitely or until discovered. As much as possible, operatives and audio teams use modern bugs that steal electricity from the building where they are planted, such as a bug placed inside a computer that looks like a small computer component or a bugged light cord that is used to replace the original.

The power source necessary will vary depending on how far the bug must transmit. The more powerful the bug's transmitter is, the more likely the bug is to be discovered. The shorter the distance the bug must transmit, the weaker the signal can be and the less detectible the bug will be. One favorite trick is to set a weak transmitter that only has to send a signal a few feet into another room where another transmitter will pick it up and amplify it. This allows the stronger transmitter to be located in a place that is unlikely to be searched or scanned with any regularity.

Bottom Line: The time a spook has and the sophistication of the target will determine who wires the space, with what, and how thorough the job is.

ALTERNATIVE INSTALLATION METHODS

Sometimes, a spook doesn't need to access a space to bug it. Many a bug has been placed by sending a nice gift to a target, such as a heavy desk clock, a lovely antique lamp, or the US Great Seal carving referenced above. The trick in these cases is to have a viable source for the gift. A contractor trying to do business with a foreign embassy might serve as such a source if the contractor is in the employ of the folks doing the bugging. Unfortunately, most of the premier targets, such as a Russian embassy, will not be easily duped into accepting gifts and placing them in secured areas. Remember—the Russians invented that trick.

In the optimum case, a targeted building will be bugged during construction. These windfalls are infrequent, but they provide the best opportunity for placing the most sophisticated, long-lasting bugs. A more frequent event would be gaining access when repair work is being done. If a spook can intercept a delivery of new furniture or appliances, they have a great opportunity to place the highest-quality bugs with well-disguised installations without setting foot on the premises.

During the Cold War, foreign diplomats, particularly Russians and Soviet Block diplomats, would come to the United States and buy gadgets—radios, TVs, answering machines, copy machines, etc. The United States would plant bugs in the equipment they purchased, often placing it inside the original packaging to make it look like it had come straight from the factory. We knew who the diplomats were and which stores they frequented, and we made sure they received the special editions straight from the vendor. This can still work today, especially with Internet shopping.

Bottom Line: Gifts and purchased items offer a wealth of opportunity for surveillance. The down side is that most countries are aware of that fact.

MONITORING BUGS

Once spooks set bugs, they must monitor those bugs. To do that, operatives and teams must have a location. An apartment or a business in an adjoining building is ideal. If the spook or team can't safely monitor the installed bug from such a nearby location, then relays can be installed to receive and retransmit the bug's signal to a different location where the spooks are set up. The operatives can also install monitoring equipment in the trunk of a vehicle. A relay can store up information. When a spook drives past the relay in a vehicle containing receiving equipment, the receiving equipment triggers the relay to transmit its stored information and recordings in a matter of seconds. Any method of picking up the transmission without being spotted is valid.

TYPES OF BUGS

Literally anything nonperishable can be bugged. Anything. Bedsteads, picture frames, crochet hooks, children's toys, Grandma's Precious Moments statuette collection, etc. Just keep in mind that anything with access to an energy source for the bug will be premium—light fixtures, switch plates, computers, printers, walls, cords, appliances, battery-operated flashlights, etc.

Anything that can be purchased from a store is also fair game, as we mentioned above.

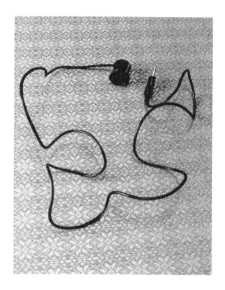

Image by Piper Bayard

This suction cup bug is from Holmes's personal collection. It's a museum piece that was out of use by 1975. Nevertheless, like many old-timers, it still has its lessons to teach.

One of the high-tech features of this bug is the suction cup itself. It is created to be used in a variety of temperatures. You may be familiar with suction cups that people can put on windows to hold little decorations. Ever noticed how they slide down the glass or just fall off when the window gets too hot or too cold? The suction cup on this bug could withstand the frosty temperatures of a winter in Moscow without budging.

The Soviets were in the habit of keeping the curtains on their safe houses closed at all times with only one exception. They would open the curtains to signal a meeting. This bug (pictured above) was great for quick bugging operations, allowing a spook to slip up to a safe house window and press it onto a corner to record those meetings.

We know what you're thinking . . . Wouldn't something that big be seen?

Sometimes. Which brings us to the next high-tech feature of this bug. It operated at a high quality while it was attached to a window or other surface. When it was pulled off of a surface, it automatically kicked down to operate at a low quality and had to be reset to the higher quality of function with an electronic code. In other words, when the Soviets found one and pulled it off the surface to study it, the bug appeared to be crap. Put that tidbit on the back burner for a moment.

The Soviet *Komitet Gosudarstvennoi Bezopanosti*, a.k.a. KGB, was the world's largest spy and state security machine with agents inside the Soviet Union and around the world focused on furthering the Soviet agenda of worldwide communism. The KGB was involved in all aspects of Soviet life, spending 75 percent of its budget to spy on the Soviet people. The Soviet *Glavnoye Razvedyvatelnoye Upravlenie*, a.k.a. GRU, was and still is Russia's main military intelligence organization. Some estimates are that the GRU has more personnel than all of the US military intelligence organizations combined. During the time of the Soviets, these organizations and others spent a great deal of time and effort spying on each other, and their bugging technology was nowhere near as advanced as that of the West.

Now take that tidbit above off the back burner. When the Soviets found this type of bug, detached it, and sent it to their labs for analysis, their scientists would tell them something to the effect of, "This bug is crap. It must be one of ours. It even has 'Made in Taiwan' printed on it." This impression of being low-tech crap diverted the Soviets from thinking that they had been surveilled by a CIA spook and instead had them thinking they were being spied on by another Soviet agency.

This particular bug was first used on the back of a refrigerator in a high-value target's home.

Wait! . . . What? Why on the back of a refrigerator?

In every culture we are aware of, people congregate in the kitchen and talk. More specific to this bug, wives of high-value targets congregated in the kitchen and talked during parties, and among those high-value wives, high-end gossip was status. They would swap tales of who was cheating, who was gambling, who had health problems, etc. This gave our spooks insights into their husbands as individuals, as well as any points of leverage for blackmail or possibly turning them to work for us.

We'd love to tell you exactly where this refrigerator was located, but the maid at the time was working as an agent for us, changing out the transmitter. She might still be alive, and we'd like to keep her that way.

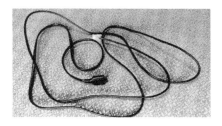

Image by Piper Bayard

This cord bug is also from Holmes's personal collection. The Soviets/Russians didn't figure this one out until around 2005.

This bug is a cord for an answering machine, and it was made for a specific installation. It is an exact replica of the original, right down to the lettering on the plastic cord, except for one difference. There are four tiny holes in each side of the business end of the cord. These tiny holes facilitate sound reaching a minute stereo microphone. This bug picked up conversations in the room as well as traffic going through the phone lines. It was powered by drawing current from the answering machine itself, and it was extremely low frequency. This made it difficult to detect with scanning equipment. The low frequency was no problem, as the bug only had to transmit as far as the janitor's closet on the other side of the wall, where another transmitter amplified the signal.

This is a perfect example of the sort of bug we mention above that can be slipped inside factory wrapping before being delivered to a surveillance target.

> **Writing Tip:** Bust out your imagination when it comes to concealing bugs. Just keep in mind the need for a power source, transmitters, and monitoring.

PINHOLE CAMERAS

The pinhole camera in history is a simple camera made from a box with a pinhole in it to let in light in lieu of a lens. Piper and others remember making them from oatmeal containers in science class as children. The name "pinhole camera" has more to do with the pinhole and the arrangement of the optics than it does with the simple box construction.

In espionage, spooks can place a digital pinhole camera inside a wall and perforate the wall with pin-sized holes to allow the camera to record the activities in the room. The camera then transmits the images to a receiver.

LASERS

Spooks might also employ an infrared laser system that bounces off the outside of windows. This is a convenient way to "bug" a room without actually having to access the space and leave something on the inside. The system is generally operated off of a small tripod, but stabilizing the system on top of a stack of books or other surface, like on a table next to a window, can work as well. The laser is directed onto the target window. A sensor in the machine picks up the vibration of the window, measures it, and translates it to the equivalent of sound with the assistance of a computer processor. These sounds can be recorded digitally, or the spook can listen to them in real time, or both.

The trickiest part of this bugging method is filtering out vibrations other than those created by the conversations, such as the vibration in the window created by a passing subway train, a heating or cooling system, or trucks chugging up and down the street. Some buildings and streets will have more of this noise than others.

The laser beam itself doesn't have to bounce back to the machine. This enables the spook to employ the laser at obtuse angles, using an optical system to read the reflection of the beam. This is handy because if the spook had to read the beam directly or have a pure partial reflection, they would be limited to narrow angles.

Because of this laser-bugging technology, in US embassies and other installations, personnel are not allowed to have any sensitive conversations near windows. Governments will put dampers in windows to partially dampen or obscure the vibrations. Also, government installations have secured chambers, such as the conference room in *Tinker, Tailor, Soldier, Spy*. Such rooms have vibration-resistant secondary foundations so that spooks can see all sides of the chamber to make sure it is clean of any surveillance equipment.

Pro Tip: When a spook travels, they might discreetly lean things against a window, like a computer bag with a shock-absorbing foam in the side. This does a great deal to dampen window vibrations during conversations. Pulling curtains can help a little, but not much. If a spook is worried about the window vibrations in a room, the better decision is to find another place to talk.

CONTACT LENS CAMERAS

As we mentioned above under Electronic Surveillance, Google and Samsung have patents for tiny cameras that can be embedded into contact lenses. They can take pictures with the blink of an eye, transmit images to electronic devices, and display images for the wearer to see. They are quite state-of-the-art, and we encourage you to dig up whatever you can find out about them on the Internet. And that is all we will say about that.

TECHNOLOGY DISTRIBUTION

The CIA and the NSA are the first to employ cutting-edge bugging technology. That's because it is their mission to collect intelligence to inform the sitting administration about foreign countries, foreign individuals, and foreign threats. Corporations end up being the second to use technology, as they are the ones who produce it. Their purposes are corporate espionage, and they are in no hurry to reveal the details of their methods.

On the other hand, the FBI and other *prosecutorial* law enforcement bodies are the last to receive espionage technology. That's because their mission is to prosecute criminals and terrorists. In the course of a prosecution, the method of collecting evidence is part of the court record. That means whatever technology is used is no longer secret. The enemies learn about it and, therefore, it is of little benefit to the CIA and the NSA.

Bottom Line: The CIA and the NSA get the best toys, then corporations, with law enforcement bodies such as the FBI coming last.

THE FIELD SPOOK'S BUGGING KIT

Once an operative gains access to a space by way of trickery, bribery, or break-in, his bugging kit need not be any larger than a paperback novel. A basic bugging kit would include bugs that can be programmed to record and/or transmit on preset schedules. The bugs can also be turned on and off remotely to foil bug sweepers. The kit would contain a small hand drill, a minimal paint kit, and epoxies for patching minute holes in walls. The paint is odor free and fast drying. For the finishing touch, the kit would contain a "puffer" for adding a layer of ambient dust to a painted area. The entire kit may be disguised in something such as a travel-size chess set or built into real cosmetic containers for a female spy or a covert cross-dresser.

ONE WAY TO PLANT A BUG

The spook first selects an advantageous location—often just above a baseboard. They begin by drilling a small hole, catching the dust on a little piece of plastic. They then select a bug from their assortment, pop it in the hole, and seal the hole with epoxy. They empty the wall dust from the hole into a baggie and then use the plastic as a palette to mix dabs of paint to match the color* of the wall. With a small brush, they paint over the epoxy and then collect all of their materials to take with them. As a finishing touch, they suck up ambient dust from against the baseboard with the puffer and puff it onto the freshly painted wall until it looks like the surrounding area.

> **Writing Tip:** Your characters' bugging efforts will be believable if you consider the full nature of the opportunities they have for surveillance and plan their bug installations accordingly. Where are they? How much time do they have? Who is the target? What equipment do they have? Work logically with your space, time, and tools, and your characters will bug like the pros.

*The necessity of being able to match colors while setting bugs is only one of the many reasons why a person with red/green color blindness won't likely become an audio specialist. On a team, there must be at least one good "painter." A spook that is color blind can still become an outstanding field operative; however, that spook is guaranteed to be last in the class on the day they learn to match paints.

13

FINDING BUGS

THE COROLLARY TO PLANTING BUGS IS FINDING THEM. THE FIRST things to consider are who is being bugged and who is doing the bugging. The sophistication of the target will determine the level of sophistication necessary to bug them successfully. The level of sophistication of the bugging job will determine the equipment necessary to detect the devices.

Mafiosi and the FBI agents that hunt Mafiosi are going to be constantly suspicious that they are under surveillance. Their wary state makes them difficult to successfully bug. That means those bugging them successfully will likely be professionals with a high level of skill. The bugs will be harder to detect, and the target will need more sophisticated equipment to detect them.

A business executive or CIA employee visiting China, Russia, or another police state would also assume that they have been targeted for surveillance, and they would sweep their hotel room or rental car routinely with electronic bug sweepers. They would also assume that they could be targeted by mobile bugging equipment when they leave their hotel. It would take a very sophisticated opponent to successfully surveil them and catch anything of importance.

If a sophisticated surveillance target does suspect a bug, the last thing they would or should do is announce it to the people around them. An intelligent person does not announce suspicions of any kind. One reason is that if the spook remains calm and quiet, they have an opportunity to discover the bug without alerting the surveillance team on the other end of it. Then they can use that bug to misinform their opponents and send them on wild-goose chases.

In contrast, most nonspook and noncriminal people go through life believing that they, themselves, really aren't that interesting. They are probably right, as professional surveillance goes, but they could still be targets of a jealous spouse or a neighborhood pervert. The good news is that the jealous spouse or neighborhood pervert is not likely to be as skilled at clandestine surveillance as an FBI agent, a CIA employee, or even the local police. Chances are good that they would use nothing more sophisticated than a NannyCam hidden in a teddy bear. Such equipment is relatively easy to detect and neutralize.

BUG SWEEPING, A.K.A. TECHNICAL SURVEILLANCE COUNTER MEASURES ("TSCM SWEEP")

A pause for terminology. "Bug sweeping" is the term that tends to be used most frequently by older spooks and spooks outside the CIA. "TSCM sweeping" is the term used by many spooks in the CIA, particularly the ones who weren't daydreaming about sex during their training. The term is also used by some younger spooks in other organizations. For our purposes, we will use the term "bug sweeping."

Spooks often have bug-sweeping devices in the field. They can be built into their phones, cameras, or other electronics and activated with a special code. As for the general public, bug-sweeping devices with various levels of sophistication are readily available at costs ranging from twenty-five dollars for a simple sweeper to fifteen hundred dollars for a sweeper with full-spectrum analysis capabilities. Anyone from spooks and criminals to nonspooks and noncriminals can readily obtain this equipment.

In the age of tiny video cameras and transmitters, we all should assume we are under video and audio surveillance. As mentioned above, finding a bug is a great opportunity for a spook to mess with an opponent, but because of this ubiquitous surveillance we all experience, a spook generally can't afford to be obvious when they sweep a room. Therefore, modern sweepers can be disguised as working cell phones that generate vibrations rather than tones. That's so the spook can pretend they are on a call and walk around a room in order to pick up any signals without arousing suspicion.

Sweepers detect transmissions from either microphones or cameras, and they do not distinguish between the two. If a spook doesn't care about tipping off the surveillance team, they can use the sweeper to zero in on the transmission and then openly inspect the vent, lamp, furniture, etc., to discover the nature of the transmitting bug. More sophisticated bugs can be remotely controlled to limit transmissions, but more sophisticated scanners can detect them even when they are not transmitting.

A sophisticated operative might wait until nighttime and use infrared detection to find heat being generated by bugs. The infrared detection method is quite effective for finding most bugs. If a spook waits a few minutes after turning off the lights to let the walls and furniture begin to cool down, they can find nearly any bug with the right sensing equipment. This is not true, though, for smoke detectors or refrigerators. Those devices can mask a bug's infrared signature, so they need to be inspected visually.

PINHOLE CAMERA DETECTION

Pinhole cameras rely on small amounts of light coming through a wall via multiple pinholes. (Refer to Pinhole Cameras mentioned earlier.) To check for a pinhole camera, a spook can turn off the lights and, while looking through an empty toilet paper tube, wrapping paper tube, mailing tube, etc., sweep the walls with a bright flashlight and watch for inexplicable small reflections. Such out-of-place light sources may indicate a pinhole camera system.

A PLAIN OLD CELL PHONE

In the absence of bug-detection equipment, a spook can be clever and use a regular cell phone to do a basic bug sweep, even if it really is just a cell phone. To do this, a spook places a call and then paces the room, listening for static to locate radio-noise sources. Such electronic noise might indicate a bug, but it might also indicate what we all already suspected—that we pay far too much for hideously low-quality cell phones. Higher-quality bugs will not be detected by a regular cell phone.

Bottom Line: All modern technology considered, one truth remains constant. That is that whether the spook is a complete innocent or a cunning old hand, the most important debugging tool they have is their brain. Equipment and techniques are fun to consider, but a clear analysis of the opponent and the situation can be more important than any technological gadgets.

14

ESSENTIAL SPOOK GADGETS

"Clothes and shoes are pretty handy if you're going out in public. Beyond that, it varies." ~ Jay Holmes

WE KNOW THIS MIGHT DISAPPOINT THE GADGET NUTS OUT THERE, but there is only one thing that a spook carries at all times, and that is their wits. Beyond that, there are exactly zero items that a spook carries at all times—not a firearm, not a bugging kit, not even a phone. The items a spook carries in their pockets, purses, or backpacks are carefully decided in each instance and depend completely on the mission. This is true of every operative and every mission.

What? Not even a gun?

Nope. In fact, sometimes carrying a gun is a sure way for a spook to blow their cover. For example, a spook might be posing as a journalist, a missionary, or a diplomat in Dublin. What happens if they get in a fender bender and have to explain to the Irish police why they have a pistol in their pocket? If the legend wouldn't carry a firearm, then they can't either.

On the other hand, if a spook's mission is to find and engage Nicaraguans that are illegally entering Honduras, it's flamingly stupid *not* to have a rifle, a pistol, grenades, well-armed friends, a radio, etc. Whether or not a spook carries a firearm is completely dependent on their legend and their mission.

There are definitely things a spook does *not* take on some missions. If they are posing as a foreigner, such as an Italian naval captain, they must be meticulous about leaving all things American behind, from their library card to their table manners. Every item they wear and carry must fit the mission and have a purpose that is designed for the success of that mission.

Bottom Line: A spook must "dress for success" with their attire, manner, and gear, and success is defined differently for every mission.

15

ESPIONAGE MYTHS

IN FICTION, THE CIA GETS BLAMED FOR EVERYTHING. IT RUNS DEEP-cover operations on American soil (*Legends*). It conducts surveillance on Americans on American soil (*Homeland*). It breaks serial killers out of prison to bump off Mexican drug lords (*The Bridge*), and it helps the Medellin Cartel to power in Mexico by assisting a Medellin Cartel hit man (*Sicario*). If that's not enough to wow you, the CIA even kidnaps infants for mind experiments that rip open the space/time continuum (*Stranger Things*).

We know exactly what you're thinking. Why doesn't everyone blame the DHS for that stuff instead of the CIA? . . . We wonder the same thing. We can only assume it's because their acronym is just not as sexy.

Due to fiction and sometimes to lax journalism, a number of myths have grown up around the CIA and other intelligence organizations. We'd like to dispel a few of those. We'll concentrate on the CIA in these espionage myths since they tend to get assigned the most extracurricular activities by those in the film and publishing industries.

MYTH 1: CIA personnel are all dangerous killers.

Actually, only a small percentage of CIA personnel are trained in the finer arts of aggression and defense, and many outstanding field operatives go through their entire lives without firing a single shot. The Company has vast and varied human resources and hires everyone from janitors to engineers to lawyers, librarians, geographers, physicists, makeup artists, tailors, etc. You name it. The CIA probably has someone to do it.

For example, the CIA has teams of construction specialists who study the building materials of countries around the world that might be logical targets of espionage. Say we are having tumultuous times with XYZistan. These construction specialists know the brand and type of switch plates used in various eras of construction in XYZistan. They come up with exact duplicates and imbed bugs. That way, the recon guy in the field can just swap out a few switch plates in a targeted space, and the job is done.

To do that requires construction specialists, plastics molders, mechanical and electrical engineers to design surveillance devices, manufacturers of surveillance devices, all of their support staff, and others, including the field operative who swaps out the switch plate in the wall in XYZistan. Most likely, only the operative in the field in this chain of people is actually trained in the finer arts of aggression and defense.

Bottom Line: "Bond" is the exception, not the rule.

Writing Tip: It's possible, and even probable, to have characters who work for intelligence organizations who are as helpless in a violent crisis as the average untrained civilian or even more so.

MYTH 2: The CIA assassinates lots of its own people.

No... Just. No.

Hollywood film producers and New York publishers kill off far more CIA operatives than the CIA ever has. This would virtually never happen in real life, no matter what the circumstances. Even if a highly trained assassin were to have a mental break and become a danger to the public, his fellows would rather see him legitimately jailed than killed. The fact is, all substantial human considerations aside, the Intelligence Community would not be able to function if it went around killing its own.

We know this for certain because Dictator Joseph Stalin of USSR fame tried it. Stalin was notorious for killing his own intelligence personnel, engineers, wives, random people in the street, etc. In fact, he had an entire branch of the KGB that was dedicated to taking out other KGB operatives. For example, Stalin several times decided the entire London office was full of bad apples, and he had almost everyone at the station purged. That doesn't leave happy, dedicated operatives in the field, nor is it a great recruitment ploy. Not that the Soviet operatives had much choice in the matter, but you get our point.

His successor, Nikita Khrushchev, backed off on this approach during his tenure as leader of the Soviet Union from 1953-1964. Leonid Brezhnev, the next dictator in the chain, finally recognized the purges were just stupid. Even KGB spookocrat Vladimir Putin is not known for killing off his own operatives, and if he can figure it out...

> **Bottom Line:** America does not and never has had any policy of killing off its own operatives. American intelligence operatives would never be the sort who blindly follow an order to take out a fellow operative. The only Americans who are that mindless and unscrupulous are in Hollywood imaginations.

Hollywood, nevertheless, has great fun with this notion. Remember the movie *RED* with Bruce Willis and Helen Mirren? The letters stood for "Retired, Extremely Dangerous." The CIA does not keep any Retired, Extremely Dangerous list. Only a Retired, Extremely Sarcastic list.

> *"There are only two kinds of retired CIA operatives—those who will continue to work for free and those who will not continue to work for free."* ~ Jay Holmes

> **Side Note:** The movie *RED* is great fun and well done. One of our personal favorites.

In fact, the CIA and the American government go to great lengths to protect their operatives and foreign agents. One excellent example of this is the Cuban Missile Non-Crisis of October 1962.

Cuban Missile Non-Crisis

Popular history in high schools and colleges across our nation and the world teaches that President Kennedy took us to the brink of nuclear war. In 1962, the USSR stationed ballistic missiles in Cuba. The United States blockaded Cuba and demanded that the Soviets remove those missiles and stop bringing in new ones. To the world, it appeared to be a game of Nuclear Chicken that could very well end up in an all-out nuclear war between the United States and the Soviet Union. However, President Kennedy was well aware of the fact that the Soviet Union was bluffing. Though its missiles in Cuba might have made it to the United States, the Soviet missiles in Russia were just as likely to misfire or fall inside Russia as they were to ever make it to an enemy target. The USSR was not capable of matching us or even coming close in a nuclear war. Nevertheless, Kennedy played along with the bluff without even telling his closest advisors.

Khrushchev, himself, did not know that the Soviet Union was not the match of the United States until we were all in the thick of it. Some poor unfortunate soul had to tell the Soviet dictator at the last minute that his cherished ICBMs were as likely to destroy Russia as they were to destroy any Western country. We have no idea how many colonels and generals in the missile program were killed for that, but we can bet it was more than a few.

So why did Kennedy play along instead of telling the Soviets to go give themselves a swirly? He did it to protect our assets in Russia.

Oleg Penkovsky

One of those assets was Colonel Oleg Penkovsky, a Soviet military intelligence officer. Penkovsky had given us specifics about the Soviet ICBMs that let Kennedy know they weren't a full-blown nuclear danger. Sadly, Penkovsky was caught by the Soviets and killed in 1963. The KGB claims he was shot. There is some evidence that this is not true. According to some sources on the inside, Penkovsky died by being by fed into a crematorium furnace, feet first, one inch at a time. That was the usual way of executing "traitors" in the Soviet Union.

Why didn't the truth come out in 1963 after Penkovsky died?

Penkovsky was not our only source at risk inside the Soviet Union, so our information reflecting the actual level of threat we faced during the Cuban Missile Crisis was kept classified until 1980.

If the truth was out in 1980, why are high schools and colleges still teaching that the Cuban Missile Crisis was such a crisis? The answer to that question is one of the most important things you can learn from this book.

Once a fiction is ingrained in popular history, it is almost impossible to effectively correct the record. It becomes accepted far and wide as "truth," and anyone who says otherwise is labeled a "conspiracy theorist" or a "nut job." Schools teach it, politics spin on it, foreign policy is set by it, and even future generations of those inside the intelligence organizations grow up not knowing any better.

This comes about for several reasons:

1. Economies invest in perceived political realities.

In the case of the Soviet Missile Not-Quite-A-Crisis, a great deal of money turned on the perceived threat level that the Soviet Union and the United States posed to each other, from the wealth of the media industries to the wealth of the military industrial complex. Once economies, and therefore societies, are invested in a "reality," perceptions of what that reality is are more important to society than any "truth" that may have occurred. Shifts in that perceived reality can jolt world markets, upend political regimes, and trigger extreme distress in coffee shops and on social media around the world.

2. Most individuals are psychologically invested in their beliefs about world events.

Where people invest their belief, so lies their world view. It's deeply disturbing to people to have it revealed that their worldview is based on lies, and people will go to great lengths to resist any new perceptions from taking root and causing them to change their views. To quote Lord Varys from *Game of Thrones*: "But what do we have left once we abandon the lie? Chaos? A gaping pit waiting to swallow us all." Few are willing to abandon their "truths" to gaze into that gaping pit.

For example, someone who grew up in the Soviet Union or the Eastern European Block countries would have been taught that the US moon landings were a vast conspiracy ... Look at the flag! It's unfurled, but there is no wind on the moon. Proof! ... Because no one would think to put a stick in the top of a flag to make it stand out, right? Nevertheless, we could literally take that person on a tour through NASA, put them in a lunar module, launch them to the moon, and bring them back, and they would still be likely to say they'd been to a movie set in Hollywood rather than revise their world paradigm. That's because the price of recognizing the truth is too high for many people. It's human nature, once a belief in the world paradigm is formed, to block out any new facts or perceptions unless their survival depends upon it, and even then, many will reject the plain information as an attack.

That's why fiction productions and publications in which truth is revealed and the entire of society sees it, accepts it, and changes its worldview on a dime, are exactly that—fiction. For example, in *Conan the Barbarian*, Schwarzenegger version, the "god" is killed in front of his slovenly followers. His people immediately line up and put out their torches and then quietly go home to live in their parents' basements again. Great movie, but that would never happen.

Far more realistic is the Harry Potter series. Rowling captures the essence of human nature when Harry returns from a battle with Voldemort and tells the truth—that the villain has returned. Do people laud Harry and get into action? Of course not. They shove their heads in the sand, label Harry a whack job, and bury the story. Better to cry "conspiracy theory" than to change the worldview in which they are psychologically and economically invested. For a realistic portrayal of what society actually does with truth, Rowling nails it.

3. The news industry doesn't write "we were wrong" articles easily or with enthusiasm.

The news industry proclaims tragedy and "tell-all" stories far and wide. Once proven false, they virtually never write a retraction unless someone sues them, and then they print it down at the bottom of whatever page comes after the legal notices. Sometimes the "retraction" is nothing more than another headline story with a great deal of spin, explaining how their journalists were really right all along, regardless of any new information to the contrary.

This is even more pronounced on social media, where the news industry produces clickbait headlines that go viral, only to tweet a retraction a few days later that almost no one sees. The retractions don't matter. Their job of promoting their agenda and raking in the cash from ads on their clickbait bunk is done. They already got their payday, and truth, apologies, and retractions are not nearly so profitable.

Bottom Line: This occurrence of popular myth trumping actual fact and becoming societal "truth" happens all the time. We'd tell you one or two, except that a) world governments, economies, societies, and individuals are heavily invested; and b) we know what happened to Harry Potter.

MYTH 3: The CIA assassinates Americans on American soil.

First off, actual assassinations, as opposed to bad days in the field, are *extremely* rare and must be authorized personally by the president. Second, those assassinations *never* target Americans on American soil. Not even if that American were a traitor of the worst magnitude. Refer to the Spook Personality, which we discussed earlier. The last thing these folks want is unconstitutional assassinations on American soil. Many of them have spent time in politically chaotic countries, and they have devoted their lives to keeping America from becoming one of those politically chaotic countries, where assassinations are common and frequently instigated by someone in government. In short, they are among those who least want America to emulate Pakistan.

Since an example is worth a thousand words...

In recent history, a foreign-born American citizen, we'll call him "Rat-bastard," was caught red-handed selling nuclear weapons designs and research data to a foreign government that enabled that government to make effective ICBMs. The Department of Justice brought over fifty charges against Rat-bastard. However, the CIA and the US administration at that time allowed him to take a plea deal for one lowly charge.

steps aside and lowers voice You know who you are, Rat-bastard. Don't even think it. You and Holmes have met before. *steps back*

Wait! . . . Why would the CIA and the US government settle for a lowly plea deal with a bona fide traitor?

Rat-bastard was an American citizen arrested by the FBI on American soil. That means he was in the US justice system, and to make charges stick would have required a trial. Trials require evidence, and part of evidence is how the evidence was obtained. If the CIA and the FBI revealed how they obtained their evidence on the traitor, our foreign assets who helped us catch Rat-bastard would be burned. Perhaps literally . . . an inch at a time.

When Rat-bastard got off on a lowly plea deal, the CIA and FBI took a firestorm of heat from the press, which, knowing nothing and caring less about legal procedure and the safety of our assets, assumed that the CIA and FBI had nothing better to do than assassinate the character of a fine, upstanding American citizen. Part of the plea deal is that Rat-bastard remains under strict surveillance by the FBI and must continue to cooperate with them. If he breaks the agreements in his deal, he will go to prison.

Hollywood and any given author would have assassinated Rat-bastard. We certainly understand the desire to do so. However, since he was an American citizen on American soil, he had rights, and those rights were respected by the CIA, the FBI, and the justice system.

Bottom Line: Intelligence organizations do not assassinate American citizens on American soil, even when they are despicable rat-bastards. Their rights will be respected by the CIA, the FBI, and the justice system.

Writing Tip: If you're going to kill a traitorous rat-bastard who is an American citizen on American soil, make sure he's forcing your protagonist's hand into self-defense. In real life, operatives do not assassinate Americans on American soil, even if they are the traitorous slime scraped off the bottom of a septic tank cleaner's shoe.

MYTH 4: The Burn Notice

Some folks have heard of something called a burn notice. In popular fiction this can range from a "You're fired!" to a contract with a hit man, but little fiction about burn notices that we've seen has any semblance to reality.

For example, in the popular TV series *Burn Notice*, Michael Westen is a CIA operative who is abandoned by the CIA after his mission goes wrong. His assets are frozen, his records are scrubbed, and he is under full-time CIA surveillance with the threat to take him into custody if he ever leaves Miami. It's a fun show, but it has exactly no basis in reality.

In real life, a "burn notice" is something used more often in Hollywood than in the IC. It is simply an alert to other agencies that someone has proven unreliable. This is so the person doesn't go from agency to agency and country to country pulling off the same con job. A real-life burn notice almost invariably regards foreign agents who are proven to be double agents. It almost never involves an American.

In the event of a burn notice, particularly on an American, no assets would be frozen. That's because the person "burned" could sue to get their assets released. Counter to popular fiction, no one gives up their rights as a citizen of the United States just because they go to work for an intelligence organization.

Also, in the over forty years Holmes has served in the clandestine services, he has *never* known of a case when any "burned" operative's movements were restricted. If there ever should be a case where an operative was confined to a specific area, that area would be someplace like Homestead, Utah, and not Miami. Miami and other large cities are full of foreign operators and criminals. The "burned" individual could easily hook up with them and indulge in shenanigans. In a place like Homestead, everyone knows everyone, and any foreigners from Russia, China, Iran, Central America, or New York City would be noticed and watched closely by everyone from the mailman to the HOA.

In *Burn Notice,* Weston's records are scrubbed, leaving him unable to obtain the necessary financial advantages of life in the West. This is true in part in that it is possible to scrub records, and the NSA is very good at it. However, if it is ever done, it is virtually always at the operative's request as a way of keeping themselves and their family safe. The scrubbing is so thorough that, once completed, it can be difficult for the operative to exercise certain basic rights that require a person to have a bit of a past. For example, an operative whose records have vanished would likely have difficulty purchasing a firearm in the United States because there would not be enough information left about them for the gun dealer to run a successful federal background check. Scrubbing has its consequences.

Keep in mind that all boundaries and norms with a burn notice can change according to the administration in charge at any time for any given reason or for no reason at all.

Bottom Line: *Burn Notice* and other such fiction is fun, but it has no basis in reality at this time.

MYTH 5: The CIA brainwashes people into being assassins.

Most of us have heard of *The Manchurian Candidate*. In it, a soldier from a political family is brainwashed to perform an assassination of a political candidate.

After the last election cycle, we know what you are asking. Why would anyone need to be brainwashed to do that? Seems like people would be lining up.

And that would be exactly the correct response.

Intelligence organizations have never needed to brainwash anyone into doing anything, particularly killing off bad guys. Think about it. Former Navy SEALs, Marine Snipers, Marine Raiders, and Army Delta Force operators are sitting around in someone's living room right now sipping whiskey and smoking cigars, talking about how they'd like to pop some of these bastards. Why on earth would the CIA or any other organization go to the trouble of brainwashing anyone when these studs would do it for free, do it right, and thank them for the opportunity?

The same also applies to breaking serial killers out of jail to do hits (*The Bridge*) and working with drug cartel hit men (*Sicario*). Why would anyone go to that kind of trouble to work with sketchy people when fine, upstanding, capable Navy, Army, and Marine operatives are available and willing?

> "It's almost as difficult to find someone to pull the trigger as it is to find air pollution in China. The problem isn't finding someone to pull the trigger. The problem is finding someone who will only pull the trigger when authorized to do so and who won't talk about it afterward." ~ Jay Holmes

Bottom Line: Neither the CIA nor any other American intelligence organization has any use for brainwashing its employees or for working with serial killers or cartel hit men.

MYTH 6: Operatives can impersonate anyone.

In the old TV series *Mission: Impossible,* Jim Phelps of Impossible Missions Force, played by Peter Graves, was given a different assignment each week, usually to unmask criminals or rescue hostages. For years he went from impersonating an East German policeman one week to a slave trader or a chemist the next. The disguises were elaborate, and the accents flawless. Sydney Bristow (Jennifer Garner) followed in this fine TV tradition in *Alias,* assuming limitless aliases to carry out missions while daylighting as a graduate student in Los Angeles. It makes for fun fiction, but real life is a bit more complicated.

In real life, deep-cover spooks live legends, also known, especially in the CIA, as "covers" or "cover stories."

It is true that some spooks can adopt wildly different covers in short periods of time, but those covers don't go especially deep, and the operations don't last long. Also, unlike Jim and Sydney, such spooks will have a limited number of covers that they can competently adopt.

For deeper missions, a spook might prepare for months, studying their legend until they know it inside out, as in, they could wake from a dead sleep and "be" that person, from answering to the name to speaking in the foreign language with the specific accent from a specific part of a foreign country. One spook we know has been out of deep cover for decades, but he still wakes from a dead sleep as his legend, and he is careful to verify the name on his passport three or four times before he hands it to an immigration officer when he travels with his family.

In order to achieve this, the spook will either have been a native speaker of that foreign language, or they will have learned the language by the age of ten so they do not speak it with an accent. But it's not just about language. The spook must also learn the colloquialisms, eating habits, mannerisms, and fashions right down to what natives carry in their pockets when they go to the store. The slightest mistake with such details could lead to capture, torture, and death.

In one famous case, an American spook during WWII was dining in a restaurant in Nazi-occupied France. There happened to be two Gestapo agents in the restaurant. They noticed him using his silverware American-style rather than European-style, and they arrested him on the spot. No doubt this brave man deserved better than for his life to serve as a warning to others, but that is how he is most remembered.

The deep-cover spook living a legend knows where they grew up, who their parents were, their parents' histories, their relatives' names and histories, where they went to school, who their friends were in school, who their lovers were, and when they first heard Meat Loaf's "Paradise by the Dashboard Light," so to speak. Their luggage and purses or backpacks will include recent pictures of "friends," and they will know every face, name, and backstory of the people in the photos. They might have an address book full of fake names, and they will be able to explain every name in the book.

> *"How do you know when you know your legend well enough? When your own mother calls you by that name."* ~ Jay Holmes

A spook can have more than one legend in a lifetime. However, because the transformation is so complete, there would rarely be a case where a spook pretends to be a Russian one week and an Afrikaner the next. There is some latitude, though, to switch between legends from countries that speak the same native language. For example, a spook who is a native French speaker could go into deep cover as a Canadian geologist at one point in their life, and at some other point in their life use a legend as a French naval officer. A great deal depends on the talents, background, and abilities of the spook involved.

Bottom Line: Living a legend takes time, training, and a spook with a rare and specific background.

Writer Tip: If part of the spook character's legend is that they are from a different country than their own, make sure that character takes on the vocabulary of the other country. For example, if your character is an American pretending they are from the UK, they should say things like "boot" instead of "trunk," "mobile" instead of "cell phone," or "bum" instead of "butt," and step up the use of "cheers" and "brilliant."

MYTH 7: Spooks use numerous complicated disguises.

Unless there is an urgency in the field, spooks don't usually do their own disguises beyond a ball cap and sunglasses. That's because if a spook uses a disguise, it's to blend in. In other words, no jungle camouflage in a suburban mall, no eye patch, and no elaborate fake facial hair. Such things only make people more noticeable.

That's not to say spooks don't employ disguises. The average field operative can handle minimal tasks such as dying hair and eyebrows or adding a simple fake scar. Some might even go so far as to have a mustache that they use on a regular basis. However, if the disguise involves altering their physical appearance beyond that, they leave that to the professional makeup artists. After all, transforming Robin Williams into Mrs. Doubtfire took some serious work by top professionals. It's no different for spooks.

Fans of *The Americans* have spent several seasons watching Russian spy Philip Jennings slip in and out of fake hair to become Clark Westerfeld as if he had some kind of magic phone booth. Clark's fake hair is so convincing he actually fools a "wife" with it when he seduces an American woman into marrying him. Great fun and all, but totally unrealistic. Not the poor duped woman part, but the disguise. While it's true the Soviets were certainly unscrupulous enough to seduce American women into fake marriages, the Soviet spies would not set themselves up for blowing their cover in these fake marriages with wigs or hair dye. No marriage gets very far without that falling apart. Even if the Soviet spies did have a magic hair phone booth, they would not create such obstacles for themselves.

Side Note: Americans did not and do not conduct "fake marriage" operations in which spooks seduce people into marriage.

Sometimes disguises are specific to purposes. For example, a spook might wear a local gas company uniform and pose as an employee in order to approach a subject in a specific location.

Another tried-and-true disguise for access is a janitor's uniform. Sometimes a spook will wear a disguise to blend in with the locals, such as specific cultural attire. And sometimes, no disguise is enough.

For example, in the Middle East and Central Asia, Westerners really stick out no matter what they wear. As a result, we need to have a great number of local assets in such places. A Pakistani on a moped can go back and forth past the same person several times without being noticed. Put a Westerner on a moped, and they'll be noticed the first or second time—it's everything from our posture to our physical appearance to the way we look at people and speak to them.

Bottom Line: Cosmetic disguises beyond simple hair dye are best left to the professionals, and some costumes should not be attempted at all.

MYTH 8: Operatives all look like James Bond or Nikita.

The majority of spooks in fiction tend to be smooth and debonair fashion pages, rocking tuxedos, leather, sports cars, and motorcycles. Bond sports a sharply-pressed tuxedo, perfect hair, and stylish cigarette cases and lighters. His boyish charm is exceeded only by his macho alpha male charisma. Nikita is a sultry slip of a woman with an extensive wardrobe of lingerie, evening gowns, and black leather. She could seduce a snake into buying its own dead skin and then kill it with her pinkie. In real life, though, spooks more often look like Walter Matthau in *Hopscotch* or Denzel Washington in *The Equalizer*. We'd give you a realistic female example, but Hollywood doesn't cast average-looking women in those roles, or many others, for that matter.

Spooks come in all shapes, sizes, colors, and charm quotients and exhibit the entire spectrum of fashion sense. For example, while Holmes's wife has occasionally wrangled him into a tuxedo, Holmes much prefers T-shirts and sweatpants to any type of suit or uniform. Another spook might only sport dresses and heels, another could be in business suits, and yet another could be in mud-covered overalls. There are as many physical and fashion varieties of spooks as there are varieties of bodies and styles.

This variety is a good thing. The cardinal rule of spookdom is that one must blend in. A tuxedo or well-tailored suit won't work in a back alley in Caracas or the Atlas Mountains in Africa, and the long-haired hippy look won't work in a five-star hotel lobby near an OPEC meeting. Field spooks must look and act whatever part they are assigned without attracting undue attention.

Bottom Line: Spooks can look like pretty much anyone, from your doctor to your neighbor . . . Yes. *Your* neighbor . . . You're thinking about your neighbor now, aren't you? If you aren't? Turn in your writer card.

MYTH 9: Operatives sleep with anything that has a pulse.

While there certainly can be promiscuous operatives, on the whole, the public would be quite surprised to discover how very conservative many spooks really are. Consider that bit in the Spook Character chapter earlier about "no drunks," "no junkies," and "no blackmail material" in the hiring process. That leads to some fairly straightlaced people in a very real way.

Another thing to think about is that most people really don't want to sleep with someone they might have to kill. Hollywood operatives don't seem to have a problem with that, but real-life spooks have hearts. Even the Russians recognized this, which we will get to in the chapter on Honeypots.

While there have certainly been booty spies over the years, it is never assumed or expected that an American operative, either man or woman, will have sex with anyone as part of an intelligence operation. If an operative is single, they might be asked if they are willing to do so, but it is definitely no black mark against them if they say no.

It is especially never assumed that a married operative will have sex with anyone during an operation. In fact, intelligence organizations rather appreciate operatives who are not eager to cheat on their spouses, even in the name of national security. If a spook is quick to cheat on their life partner, their character might be something to question. Also, such promiscuity could leave operatives vulnerable to blackmail, as well as some seriously exotic crotch fleas. When sex is needed for an operation and none of the operatives is up for it, the Company has well-developed relationships with local madams and high-class prostitutes who are ready and willing to step up.

Bottom Line: There is more than one way to skin a banana, so to speak, and operatives are just like the rest of the population in getting to choose their partners. And like the rest of the population, some operatives will choose more partners than others.

Writing Tip: Instead of having your character seduce a foreign operative, have him or her come up with creative ways to avoid having sex with the enemy seducer.

MYTH 10: Operatives always order room service.

Yeah . . . What's with that? You'd think Bond would have learned by the second movie, *From Russia With Love*, that hotel staff in the room often ends badly. But he just keeps ordering room service. Perhaps we should send the Screenwriters Guild a copy of this book?

Bond is not the only guilty party. In the otherwise realistic *Act of Valor*, two spooks order out for Chinese while sitting in a Third World country. What could possibly go wrong with that? Of course, one is killed and the other gets snatched and tortured.

In real life, field spooks don't order room service or delivery of any kind while they are on a mission. At least if they're smart and they like staying alive, they don't. In fact, Holmes won't even call for a pizza to be delivered when he is home in the States. Even most restaurants give him hives, and he only genuinely enjoys his wife's entrées, his own, and Piper's chocolate cakes. That's because one of the easiest ways to gain access into someone's space and poison or otherwise kill them is through room service, food service, or food delivery. It's right up there with home improvement crews, electrical repair crews, and the cable guys who only ever show up at the end of the day. Field spooks know this because they use those tricks themselves to gain access to targets.

> **Bottom Line:** Field spooks generally don't order room service and are loathe to allow strangers into their space, whether on a mission or at home, because they know those tricks.

Writing Tip: Instead of elaborate schemes to break into someone's home, office, or hotel room, have your characters gain access into someone's home as the pizza delivery person, the Amazon delivery person that can open subscribers' doors, or the cable guy. Just make sure that if they're posing as the cable guy, they're five hours late, or they'll blow their cover. The real spooks always prefer to do what is easiest with the least amount of fuss or potential gunfire, and often that means *deception rather than force.*

MYTH 11: Every mission includes a gunfight or a cruise missile.

In real life, spooks prefer to avoid gunfights wherever and whenever possible. Bad days happen. No one wants to create a bad day where one doesn't need to exist. Also, the minute someone takes a shot, or things "get loud," the spook's cover is blown. It's worth quoting again . . .

"You're only covert until the first shot is fired." ~ Jay Holmes and Every Other Field Spook Since the Dawn of Firearms

In truth, a great deal of fieldwork is about collecting intelligence and surveillance, even when the World's Most Wanted are the targets. One example of this type of fieldwork is the hunt for Carlos the Jackal.

Billy Waugh and Carlos the Jackal

Ilyich Ramirez Sánchez, a.k.a. Carlos the Jackal, was born to a millionaire communist lawyer in Venezuela on October 12, 1949. Funded by both Saddam Hussein and Moammar Gadhafi, Carlos was responsible for multiple bombings, assassinations, and hostage takings throughout the 1970s and 1980s.

His most well-known attack occurred at a meeting of the Organization of the Petroleum Exporting Countries ("OPEC") in 1975 in Vienna. Carlos and his team took seventy hostages, killed three people in the process, and kidnapped eleven oil ministers. He then commandeered a plane and took his captives to Algiers, where he released them in exchange for twenty million USD. Carlos kept ten million of that and gave the rest to the Popular Front for the Liberation of Palestine.

The following year, he was involved with the Palestinian hijacking of a French plane bound for Entebbe, Uganda—the same hijacking featured in *Raid on Entebbe* that ended in an Israeli commando raid. Carlos claimed he was inspired by both communism and Palestinian liberation movements, but we suspect he is more like the vast majority of terrorists—a depraved, egomaniacal dirtbag who'll pin himself on any excuse to act like a depraved, egomaniacal dirtbag.

Fortunately, we have Billy Waugh on our side, and Billy is a master of tracking down depraved, egomaniacal dirtbags.

Billy Waugh is a true Badass. He is a Badass's Badass. He's such a Badass he would *never* call himself a Badass because he's also a very modest, unpretentious man. Like all true Badasses, he is the first to insist he's no hero.

We could write an entire book about Billy Waugh that wouldn't even scratch the surface of his badassery, but we don't have to. We highly recommend you read *Hunting the Jackal,* which is Waugh's autobiography of his service in the US Army Special Forces and the CIA from the Korean War through his tracking and surveillance of Osama bin Ladin and the capture of renowned terrorist Carlos the Jackal in 1994. The book's preface starts with

Waugh's seventy-second birthday, December 1, 2001, when he was in the wilds of Afghanistan. He jumped in to hunt down the Taliban and Al-Qaeda. . . . When he was seventy-two. . . . Yeah. Just get the book.

In December of 1993, at the age of sixty-four, Billy Waugh traveled to Khartoum, Sudan, a.k.a. K-town, for the purpose of leading a four-man team in the hunt for Carlos the Jackal. At the time, Billy had the suspicion that underneath the terrorist legend, he would find a shallow mercenary, or what we would call a dirtbag. In addition to his epic acts of terrorism, Carlos was known for drunken debauchery, womanizing, and having his ego heavily invested in his Robin Hood persona and global notoriety. Waugh suspected Carlos's lifestyle would catch up to him. Waugh's instruction upon arriving in Khartoum was to find Carlos the Jackal. No problem, right? He had a ten-year-old photograph and only a million people in Khartoum to sort through.

After over two weeks spent scouring the streets of K-town, they caught a break. Carlos called one of his bodyguards and instructed the man to come to Khartoum. The call was picked up by the field station where the bodyguard was staying, and the information made it back to Waugh and his team.

The team set up watch on the airport. However, when the bodyguard arrived, he was secreted out of the area. Nevertheless, Waugh and his team knew what the bodyguard looked like, and as a large Caucasian with wavy white hair, he was more likely to frequent certain areas of the city over others. Waugh and a man he calls "Greg" went to dinner at Le Meridian Hotel, one of the locations frequented by Caucasians in Khartoum. They had only gone for dinner, but as they were leaving through the lobby, they caught sight of the bodyguard. Waugh and Greg kept walking and waited outside to scope out his vehicle, which turned out to be a white 1990 Toyota Cressida with a Khartoum civilian license plate. They weren't able to follow it long without losing it in the rush of the Khartoum streets, but they were closing in.

Waugh and his team spent sixteen hours per day, every day, looking for the white Cressida in the streets of Khartoum. They concentrated their efforts in areas that would appeal to a playboy boozer. The approach paid off. On the first Thursday in February 1994, Greg and a man called "Don" spotted the Cressida at the Diplomatic Club and followed it. Though they lost the vehicle, it was not before Waugh obtained enough information to narrow down the vehicle's destination to a neighborhood called the New Addition.

For the next six days, sixteen hours a day, Waugh and his team searched for the Cressida at the New Addition and the surrounding area. Then, on the afternoon of February 8, Don spotted the vehicle parked adjacent to the Ibn Khaldoun Hospital in the New Addition. Waugh and Greg rushed over from the US Embassy, where they had been in the photo lab. They parked twenty meters from the Cressida where Waugh would have a clear shot with his Canon 35mm camera. Greg walked across the street to a cigarette vendor, and Waugh got out and raised the hood of his Land Cruiser, pretending he was having engine trouble in order to give himself and Greg a visible reason to be parked there. Then Waugh got back into the Land Cruiser and readied his camera with the lens focused on the exit door of the hospital. They waited.

Suddenly, Carlos's young wife appeared in the view of the lens and walked toward the Cressida. Greg immediately began a loud argument with the cigarette salesman while Waugh snapped pictures of the woman. Then a man who could have been Carlos the Jackal himself appeared with another man at the hospital door and walked toward the Cressida, distracted by Greg's argument with the vendor. The men stopped to stare, and Waugh took numerous pictures. Then the men followed the woman to the Cressida, got in, and drove away. Greg finished his argument with the vendor by passing him twenty USD, and then Waugh and Greg drove back to the embassy to develop the film while Don followed the Cressida to a gated apartment complex on Thirty-Fifth Street.

The pictures were couriered to Washington, DC and to Jordan for positive identification. It was, indeed, Carlos the Jackal.

Waugh suggested that they save the US taxpayers a great deal of money by offing Carlos and pinning it on some other government that wanted him even more—a most sensible plan by Bayard & Holmes's calculations. However, that was quashed right away. Instead, they were told to stay back, that they were not allowed to surveille the Jackal until further notice. The chief of station was concerned that too much activity would alert Carlos to the fact that he had been found.

On February 19, Waugh was ordered back to the United States, and he spent the next two months flying four trips back and forth to Africa. During part of that time, they received a tip that Carlos was on the move to Cairo, and Waugh was sent to the Cairo airport for six mind-numbing days of watching for the Jackal. It turned out to be a red herring. Waugh returned to Khartoum and suggested to his boss that he find a good operating position from which to watch and photograph Carlos. Waugh's boss agreed.

At the end of May, after over two months of searching for the right location to set up surveillance, Waugh found a decrepit sixth-floor apartment two blocks from Carlos's residence. It had a full, clear field of vision to the front gate of Carlos's apartment. Waugh and Greg paid the owner the usurious rate of seven hundred dollars/month for three months up front and moved in 300 pounds of camera equipment during the night—up six flights of stairs. One of their goodies was a state-of-the-art camera lens that weighed 140 pounds and measured two feet across.

The apartment itself was beyond condemning by American standards. The floor was buried in trash and crap, as in crap. There was no running water and no bathroom facilities. Their makeshift "bathroom" was a coat closet that happened to have an open pipe that simply led downward. They cooked rice on a Bunsen burner and ate military rations. They covered the windows with thin black material. Waugh and his team alternated twenty-four-hour shifts for the next three months, photographing everyone who went in and out and recording all activity in a book at the US Embassy.

This was all well and good, but Waugh didn't have permission to take out the dirtbag, and the United States didn't have an active warrant on Carlos. But the French did. At the end of July, Waugh's boss, Cofer Black, met with Philippe Rondot, who was not only the head of the French Direction de la Surveillance du Territoire ("DST"), but also a man with a vendetta against Carlos. As the United States hoped, the French detained Carlos the Jackal on the night of August 12, 1994, and took him back to France.

Carlos was put on trial and convicted of murdering a French informant and two French counterintelligence agents. At the time of publication, he was still incarcerated at Clairvaux Prison, serving a life sentence.

And Billy Waugh? He is still alive and well at the time of publication. Like we said—a Badass's Badass. You can find out more about Billy in our upcoming release, *Key Figures in Espionage: The Good, the Bad, and the Booty*, but that's no substitute for reading *Hunting the Jackal*, so we recommend Billy's book, too.

> **Bottom Line:** Field missions are more often about long periods of clandestine observation than they are about gunfights or cruise missiles.

MYTH 12: Spooks drop their guns when hostage takers yell, "Drop the gun!"

Now we get to Piper's pet peeve. It seems obligatory in crime and espionage thrillers that at some point, the protagonist rushes in, and the antagonist grabs someone, points a pistol at them, and says, "Drop your gun, or I'll shoot!" Invariably, anywhere from a single spook to entire rooms full of police and FBI agents drop their weapons.

Meanwhile back at the ranch, Piper is throwing a shoe at the TV and yelling, "Shoot the bastard! My ten-year-old could make that shot!"

No spook or FBI agent is going to drop their weapon unless they are surrounded with multiple weapons trained on them. The only thing that would happen if they did drop their weapons is that they would be killed along with the hostage. Depending on the rest of the circumstances when faced with the "Drop the gun" scenario, an operative will most likely take the shot. And make it.

Spooks involved in more kinetic operations have to practice regularly. And have you ever noticed how much of the antagonist's head and body are almost invariably hanging out in the breeze when the bad guys do this? Give a range-qualified spook or FBI agent a forehead to aim at, and that antagonist is toasted.

Maybe up close, you might say, but not from across a large room.

To that we would answer, define "up close." Piper once asked Holmes the maximum distance he would be comfortable shooting a terrorist with a pistol if that terrorist was holding a child in front of his torso with only the terrorist's forehead and eyes visible. Holmes's answer? Forty yards without a silencer.

Granted, Holmes is the Yoda of combat pistol. (Piper put that in. Holmes would object, as he is quite modest. Piper would object to his objecting. None of that objecting would change the truth of the matter.) But you get the idea. Using a "meat shield" is not a Get-Out-of-Jail-Free Card in real life like it is on TV and in the movies.

Some of you may recall back in 2009 when Somalian pirates seized a cargo ship, the *Maersk Alabama,* and took Captain Phillips hostage. After days of verbal dancing, there came a point when three pirates held Captain Phillips in a lifeboat with a gun at his back as the USS *Bainbridge* towed the boat forty yards behind. Three US Navy SEALs took coordinated head shots at the three Somali pirates, killing them simultaneously, while carefully making sure that none of the bullets passed through a pirate to hit Captain Phillips. Yeah. That's how the "I've got a hostage, drop the gun" thing often plays out in real life.

We can hear the Jack Reacher fans from here ... But wait! Jack is always throwing down all of his weapons and getting into fistfights.

Far be it from us to criticize a great like Lee Child. Just be aware that Jack Reacher is a fictional character, and he has a really good thing going—for a fictional character. Go, Jack, go! But don't try that at home or anywhere else in the real world. That's because in the real world ...

> *"If you're in hand-to-hand combat, you've already done something wrong."* ~ Jay Holmes

> **Bottom Line:** A spook doesn't need a big target, and dropping their gun will only get them killed along with any hostages.

MYTH 13: The Long Good-bye

We've all seen the Bond movies where the villain has Bond at gunpoint, or on a table with a laser about to cut him in half, or chained with a woman in a bikini over a shark pit, and a long conversation ensues. The villain explains his motives, his mechanisms, his future goals, how his mother always gave his brother the last cookie, when his first dog died, etc. They exchange pithy quips with Bond before leaving him to die, and Bond uses some cute gadget or handy space heater to get out of the situation. Equally common are the long soliloquies while a protagonist holds someone else at gunpoint.

No... Just. No.

In real life, a spook always has to be aware not only of the enemy in front of them, but who will be coming through the door next. Bad guys rarely work in a vacuum. They tend to collect an entourage of other bad guys, clingers, wannabe bad guys, and friends of friends who hope to earn the new leather jacket they just put on a credit card to impress their girlfriends. In other words, a real spook never takes for granted that the situation is under control. They want it over, and they want to get out of there. If the goal is a kill, they get it done.

> **Bottom Line:** No one gets a long good-bye. In the field, when a spook has the shot, they take it.

16

HONEYPOTS AND THE HONEYPOT ASSASSIN

"Dating for me was gorgeous Russian women appearing out of nowhere and pretending to love me, and me pretending to believe them." ~ Jay Holmes

HONEYPOTS ARE SPIES TRAINED TO USE SEX FOR THE PURPOSE OF wheedling information out of targets, luring targets to specific locations, and/or enticing targets into behavior that can be used to blackmail them. These professionals are highly skilled in the arts of seduction and pleasure, and they will perform literally any act the target desires.

One of the most common myths in fiction is that of the Honeypot Assassin—the seductress who murders her mark in the name of espionage. We won't say it never happens in real life, but it pretty much doesn't happen on purpose. This goes back to the fact that most people aren't black widow spiders. As a general rule, we humans like to keep our killing and our sex compartmentalized far away from each other. Even the Soviets recognized this.

The seductive love-kitten personality and the assassin personality are fundamentally different from each other—a rather universal fact. For example, the assassin will likely balk at the simple act of surrendering their hair to a barber for a trim. Honeypots, on the other hand, must freely surrender their entire bodies to total strangers. Not only that, the honeypot must be convincingly enthusiastic about doing absolutely anything the target wants him or her to do, even if it involves a troupe of circus acrobats, random vegetables from the grocery produce section, flying monkeys, dirty shoes, or inappropriate references to their mother and barnyard animals. In fact, the more elaborate, exotic, or outright depraved the target's behavior, the better for the honeypot. Since honeypots are most frequently about obtaining blackmail material, vanilla sex is of virtually no use to them. Their goal is to lure the target to their prewired lair to extract and live out the mark's deepest, darkest fantasies.

Honeypots work with teams that go into a space ahead of them and set up whatever surveillance equipment is appropriate to the task at hand. It's the honeypot's job to get the mark back to that space for the soirée with the flying monkeys, so to speak. In the rare case that the goal *is* assassination, the honeypot will most commonly lure the target to a specific location for someone else to take over from there.

Bottom Line: While we won't say there are *never* honeypot assassins, they would be freakishly rare and mental to some degree.

Honeypots don't just target spooks. Spooks are actually the minority targets. Any businessman, senator, banker, engineer, scientist, or person in a position to potentially know something of value is a viable mark. Honeypots from various countries target these marks in coffee shops, museums, bars of five-star hotels, or any other place where they can strike up a conversation that quickly leads to, "What is the dirtiest thing you have ever wanted to do? I want to do it with you."

> *"How do you know if there's a honeypot working your Moscow hotel? You're in a Moscow hotel."* ~ Jay Holmes

Honey traps don't work on every target, but they work frequently. If they didn't work, the Russians and other countries would not waste millions of dollars in such enterprises. The Russians may not be "Soviet" anymore, but they are still the same cheap spies that they were a few decades ago, and they don't like wasting money that could be better spent on misappropriations for their own personal use.

Americans have never used as many honeypots as Russia and other countries do. As we mention in the Espionage Myths chapter, while there have been American booty spooks over the years, no American intelligence operative is ever expected to have sex with anyone as part of a mission. The American IC keeps a Rolodex of high-level prostitutes ready to meet any such requirements. The Russians, on the other hand, keep a large stable of honeypots, and they always have. No doubt some Russian honeypots are volunteers. However, many, particularly during the Cold War, are beautiful women and men who have been coerced into the profession with threats of harm to their families.

Anna Chapman and JFK

Perhaps the most famous honeypot of recent times is Russia's Anna Chapman. Chapman was arrested in New York City in June of 2010 after accepting a fake passport from an undercover FBI agent and agreeing to pass it on to a third party. Chapman, a.k.a. Anna Vasilyevna Kushchenko, was subsequently deported to Russia with nine other members of her spy ring in an exchange for four Americans who were being held captive there for spying. Russia received them back with open arms, and Anna Chapman became an overnight celebrity in her homeland, enjoying magazine cover photo shoots and visits with Putin—as much as one could ever enjoy a visit with Putin, that is.

Allegations have been made that Chapman had been in contact with a member of President Obama's cabinet. However, no one has offered up any claims of wrongdoing by the mysterious cabinet member in question. While we don't know whether she got close to a cabinet member or whether she or the cabinet member or both had their clothes off in any sort of "too closeness," we do know that this sort of thing is possible.

Some of the more interesting honeypot cases that have slowly leaked over time involved US President John F. Kennedy. Since his assassination, it has been well documented that JFK was rather sexually active outside of his marriage. President Kennedy and his brother, US Attorney General Robert Kennedy, took breaks from their work by hosting nude pool parties for young women. The list of famous women who have since claimed to have slept with President Kennedy includes several dozen actresses and celebrities. He also holds the distinction of having slept with three honeypots, though not simultaneously, and not all while he was president.

One of the spies, Inga Arvad, was ostensibly working for the Nazis during WWII when JFK slept with her. The second occurrence was during Kennedy's presidential trip to Ireland, when he apparently slept with a Soviet spy. That spy was later involved with the British "Profumo Affair," which brought down the government of British Prime Minister Harold Macmillan. In a third incident, JFK slept with a member of a freelance spy ring who was selling information on a "piecework basis" to Russia and its Warsaw Pact allies. In spite of this busy sex schedule with foreign spies, there is no credible evidence that JFK shared any secret information with any of his seemingly countless conquests.

And that's the other side of the honeypot equation. Getting a man; or a woman; or a man, a woman, and a flock of flying monkeys into bed; and getting he, she, or them to share some bodily fluids; does not always lead to obtaining useful information. For all of Anna Chapman's fame in the West and her Russian hero status at home, it seems that she gave Russia little more than a bit of humorous PR value.

When operatives have missions in locations where the Russians, Chinese, or others have an abundance of honeypots, the operatives must take all of those eyes and ears into account. One way an intelligence agency can deal with all of those spies is to do what's called "flood the local environment." That means sending out a bevy of spooks to attract the attention of the honeypots, their surveillance teams, and any other spies in the area and keep them busy.

This tactic has numerous uses. Operatives might flood the environment to keep enemy spies averted while an important mission goes down elsewhere in the area. It's an espionage sleight of hand, if you will. Another reason operatives will flood the environment is to assess the quantity and behavior of another country's spooks—to find out how enemy teams will react to the flood, and how many teams might be working in a particular area. And sometimes, American operatives will flood the environment just to fake out the other side and mess with their heads.

When operatives are sent out to flood the environment, there is no hard-and-fast rule as to how a spook might keep the honeypot occupied. A single operative is certainly welcome to partake of the honeypot's charms and skills in such a case. A more conservative operative or one who is married might find creative ways to avoid actual physical intimacy, such as visiting tourist sites and making the honeypot think they're really turned on by walking twenty miles a day and stopping for gelato every ten minutes. There is no formula, only the response in the moment, and it's up to the skills and wits of the field spooks to handle the situation.

> **Writing Tip:** For a fun twist, have an operative who does *not* want to sleep with an enemy target have to come up with creative ways of avoiding intimacy while holding the attention of the honeypot and her surveillance team.

Honeypots aren't always working directly for a government like Holmes's dates were during the Cold War. Sometimes they are prostitutes who are working with a pimp that uses them to gather information in order to sell it to the highest bidder, or several bidders. We can't be certain that the prostitutes in the Fat Leonard Conspiracy we discuss in the Conspiracies section were acting as honeypots, pumping these idiots—if you'll pardon the pun—for information so Fat Leonard could sell it to our enemies and to criminal organizations. We *can* be certain, however, that Fat Leonard probably would not have missed that trick . . . So to speak.

> *"The most humiliating failure for any spook is to get caught by a honeypot. It would mark the spook as the Pee-wee Herman of the spook world."* ~ Jay Holmes

Learn more about Honeypots in our upcoming release, *Key Figures in Espionage: The Good, the Bad, and the Booty.*

ELECTRONIC HONEYPOTS

Some people may be more familiar with the term "honeypot" as applied to the cyberverse rather than to HUMINT. An electronic honeypot is a decoy set up to detect intruders into systems and to collect information on them. We are not cybersecurity experts, so we asked Chris Magill to define honeypots for you. As you may recall from the chapter on Electronic Surveillance, Chris is an Information Security Professional and privacy advocate who helps companies manage their cryptographic systems and hunting down hackers.

"A 'honeypot system' or a 'honeypot server' can either be as complex as entire servers or as simple as a virtual machine with known vulnerabilities. They are typically generic, but sometimes tempting false data files can be left to trick an attacker into thinking they've found something of value or to help prove attribution later if those same files show up in the wild. They are also frequently used as part of an intrusion detection system ('IDS'), since legitimate business users would have no business accessing that machine." ~ Chris Magill

Honeypot systems are not substitutions for other forms of cybersecurity. They are decoys for the purpose of learning how intruders are able to attack networks and for collecting the information necessary to catch those intruders. As we noted, we are not cyber experts. Therefore, we'll just point you to an article that Chris Magill recommends for an excellent overview of the topic: *Honey Pot Systems Explained* by Loras R. Even, (Boston, MA: SANS Institute, July 12, 2000).

17

CONSPIRACIES

Yes. They are real. Not all of them, but definitely some of them, and they've been around since Adam and Eve partnered up with a snake and tried to pull one over on God.

"Conspiracy" is defined by the *Oxford English Dictionary* as "A secret plan by a group to do something unlawful or harmful." It's a very popular word these days, as it's used in the term "conspiracy theory," which is the label politicians place on pretty much anything they want to discredit. However, pick up any political history book, and it will be full of conspiracies. They don't stop just because our party, our candidate, or our friends or neighbors get into office. In fact, we challenge anyone who dismisses "conspiracy theories" as automatic nonsense to tell us exactly what date in history they believe conspiracies ceased to exist.

That being said, many conspiracy theories out there are complete nonsense. We'd point out that sometimes a cigar is just a cigar, but that might make us appear to have been involved in a twentieth-century Freudian conspiracy. So moving right along . . . For example, there's an entertaining conspiracy theory out there right now that the CIA has their own large bunker complex underneath the Denver International Airport, complete with an underground traffic tunnel stretching all the way back to D.C. . . . Because that's so much easier and more efficient than just catching one of the planes directly above them at the airport. Sheesh!

Are intelligence operatives ever involved in conspiracies? Yes. But only in conspiracies that are sanctioned by Congress and/or the president against our enemies or on behalf of US interests abroad. Intelligence operatives, politicians, former politicians, military officers, or any other citizens of the United States who are involved in conspiracies that are not sanctioned by Congress and/or the president for the best official interests of the United States are by definition criminals.

Sadly, at the time this book is being written, the US Navy is caught in the throes of one of those latter conspiracies. In fact, it is the greatest known American military corruption conspiracy of this century to date—the Fat Leonard Conspiracy. There are a few absolutes in life . . . Don't pee on an electric fence. Don't send money to a Nigerian prince. And don't ever do business with anyone named "Fat Leonard."

After a three-year investigation, the story first broke in November 2013 with the accusation that Director of Naval Intelligence Vice Admiral Ted "Twig" Branch and four other naval officers accepted bribes of cash, prostitutes, and expensive trips in exchange for steering US Navy contracts for port services to a company named Glenn Defense Marine Asia ("GDMA"). Indictments started coming down.

Several naval officers and civilians were arrested at that time on charges of Conspiracy and Bribery. Among those arrested was the apparent mastermind, one Leonard Glenn "Fat Leonard" Francis, a Malaysian businessman who was the owner and CEO of

GDMA. He was a port service kingpin in the South Pacific region with alleged connections to Communist China. According to the US Justice Department prosecutors, "This is the first time multiple officers are charged as working all together in a multi-layered conspiracy, pooling their individual and collective resources and influence on behalf of Francis." It is a multilayered conspiracy with countless cost to our nation.

One of the indictments was unsealed on March 14, 2017, and its seventy-eight pages reveal just how extensive this maze of betrayal, greed, debauchery, and arguably even treason had become, involving at least twenty US Navy officers including a vice admiral, five rear admirals, a Marine colonel, five Navy captains, six Navy commanders, two Navy lieutenant commanders, and a Navy warrant officer, along with several top GDMA employees. Some officers even drew their wives into this proven criminal conspiracy. The indictment includes charges of Conspiracy, Bribery, False Statements, and Obstruction of Justice, and Conspiracy to Commit Honest Service Fraud—a laundry list of what *not* to do as a naval officer.

It began in January of 2006 when Navy Contract Supervisor Paul Simpkins, a Department of Defense civilian employee, contacted Fat Leonard and offered to throw Navy ship docking service contracts to GDMA in exchange for cash. One month later, the cash—*our* taxpayer dollars—started flowing. GDMA signed a $929,000 contract with the US Navy for docking services. Not only was this the first contract of many, but the Navy now estimates that it paid more than double the normal rate for the services provided. In exchange, Simpkins received $50k in US cash from Fat Leonard's grubby, chubby hands.

In short time, Simpkins and Fat Leonard pulled several naval officers into their dealings—senior officers who were responsible for coordinating missions, directing operations, directing ship movements, and scheduling port visits to service the ships and submarines of our US Navy Seventh Fleet, which is the US Far Eastern Fleet. One conspirator was even the commanding officer of the nuclear aircraft carrier USS *George Washington*.

Soon, these senior US Navy officers were using their positions and influence to direct business to Fat Leonard's facilities throughout the Far East. Not only that, some of the officers regularly sent the Malaysian *classified ship schedules* and helped protect GDMA from investigations by the Naval Criminal Investigative Service ("NCIS").

In return, the officers received lavish dinners, time with prostitutes, expensive gifts, travel expenses, and luxury hotel accommodations for themselves and their families. Needless to say, it is *highly* illegal for *any* government employee, military or civilian, to receive such largesse from defense contractors or any other influencers. Not only that, Fat Leonard was a Malaysian national operating a multimillion-dollar business throughout the Far East, including facilities in Hong Kong.

You know, Hong Kong? That place controlled by Communist *China*, the hostile country that spies on the US at every possible opportunity? Yeah. That Hong Kong. Because a Malaysian criminal defrauding the US government is certainly going to be too moral and ethical to trade or sell our classified information to his host country of China, right?

We don't claim to know to what extent Fat Leonard or any of the implicated GDMA employees are involved with the Communist Chinese government or with individuals who are involved with that government. By exposing our ships to service employees from foreign docking and ship services that were operated by a criminal, these US Navy conspirators unduly exposed our technology to those who would do us damage—individuals possibly working on behalf of Communist China. We may never know if the Communist Chinese government received classified information about the highly sensitive systems on our US Navy vessels, but it would be an unusual misstep for the Chinese if they did not.

That senior Navy officers and Navy Criminal Investigation Division agents willingly helped schedule and then attended wild parties in Hong Kong, Malaysia, and the Philippines, where they were serviced by prostitutes procured by GDMA indicates a frighteningly amateurish level of conduct by trained professionals. Did the Communist Chinese government conduct honeypot operations against these Navy officers with the help of GDMA? We can't say for certain, but it's entirely plausible and a good bet. If Holmes were Chinese, he certainly would not have missed the opportunity for such an easy intelligence coup.

At the time of publication of this book, civilian courts had indicted thirty suspects, and the US Navy says it has substantiated misconduct on the part of approximately fifty people so far. For a more detailed account of the referenced indictment, see Bayard & Holmes: US Navy, Fat Leonard, and the Military Corruption Conspiracy of the Century at http://bayardandholmes.com/2017/04/05/us-navy-fat-leonard-and-the-military-corruption-conspiracy-of-the-century/. For the foreseeable future, the conspiracy will continue to unfold, and the indictments will continue to flow.

Bottom Line: Conspiracies are alive and well to varying degrees in military and political circles, just as they possibly are in your own local law enforcement and your own HOA. Making them public and labeling them "conspiracy theories" does not nullify the fact that they are, indeed, conspiracies.

Writing Tip: When it comes to writing conspiracies, don't be shy. Politics are global, commerce is global, and communications are global—the Great Triumvirate of Big Politics, Big Money, and Big Media. That's all that's necessary for Big Conspiracies. Just be sure any conspiracies you write get labeled publicly as "conspiracies" so the public will ignore them.

18

SLEEPER AGENTS

MANY OF US ARE FAMILIAR WITH *THE AMERICANS*, WHICH IS A SHOW about undercover KGB agents posing as Americans in the DC area during the Cold War. They run multiple operations at a time, work as everything from honeypots to assassins to thieves and grave robbers, and they receive frequent phone calls at home where they live with their children from "The Center." Their covers have covers, and they slip in and out of various roles and disguises as if there's no chance of ever running into their kids' teachers at the grocery store. The man of the couple pops in and out of a wig and facial hair so adeptly that the poor woman he dupes into a fake marriage doesn't notice it's not real. They even have a daughter they work at pulling into the "family business." Basically, Philip and Elizabeth Jennings are the one-stop shop for all of the Soviets' espionage needs. It's a very fun show. It has virtually no basis in reality.

The Soviets had honeypots, assassins, thieves, surveillance teams, sleeper agents, etc. The Russians still do. But even the Russians don't expect their spies to be jacks-of-all-trades. Real Russians planted into American society under deep cover for the long term are serious investments, both financially and in terms of personnel. These high-value operatives would never be used for such a variety of mundane tasks as assassinations, running agents, robbing laboratories, etc. And the thirty-second disguise that fools a spouse? Hollywood is once again holding out on the government if they've got that one.

Bottom Line: Any Russians passing as Americans who were active agents during the Cold War, as opposed to sleeper agents, were certainly never used so broadly and recklessly as are the imaginary Philip and Elizabeth Jennings on *The Americans*.

Far more common during the Cold War were Soviet sleeper agents. In real life, the Soviets were experts at developing and planting deep-cover sleeper agents into American society. While some agents born in Eastern Bloc countries may have been trained for a few years and slipped in to "make connections," Soviet children, in some cases, were literally trained from birth for their roles.

The Soviets created entire towns that simulated America. It has long been known in the West and denied by the Russians that our Korean War POWs were sent to the Soviet Union. We believe many of them were coerced into helping perfect the Soviet efforts to replicate American life in these towns.

The towns' occupants spoke American English, and society was as close to genuine American society and life as the Soviets could make it. Children were born there, or children were taken there at a very young age. Entire families with young children moved to these towns. Many grew up never speaking Russian, never seeing a Soviet city, and never being acquainted with Russian society or traditions more than an American would be. Culturally, they ate American food, played American games, and attended "American" schools. The goal was to create agents that could seamlessly slip into American society.

The Soviets went to these great lengths to train these sleeper agents because during the Cold War, actual Russians coming to America were closely watched by the American IC, the neighbors, the postman, the clerk at the corner store, etc. The Soviets needed Russian operatives that could fit in and be unobtrusive. Soviet spies from other countries, such as East Germany, did not have to pretend to be Americans. They were not as rare or as suspect as their Russian counterparts so the Soviets had more latitude with training and constructing their legends.

Once the Soviet spies were prepared to live their legends in the United States, they were prepped to do one job, and one job only. That would be to sabotage a specific bridge, poison a specific water supply, destroy a specific overpass, take out a specific dam, etc. Once prepared, they were inserted into America to begin their real American lives. They established themselves near their specific target, lived as normal Americans in their communities, and "slept" until the day they would receive the order to carry out their mission should the Soviet Union and America go to war.

So how were these sleeper agents able to establish themselves near their targets?

Sometimes sleeper agents accomplished this as easily as purchasing a home in a community, perhaps along with a small store or gas station. They would set up shop as a young couple or young family that was starting over in a new town. Sometimes, say if a gas station was located near a crucial overpass in the middle of nowhere, the owners of that station would have fatal accidents or a robbery/homicide would occur, opening up an opportunity for a new owner to buy the place. "The Americans" would move in, have children, raise families, and wait. The Soviets were very good at this.

Americans, on the other hand, were never good at planting sleeper agents inside Russia or anywhere else. Counter to popular fiction, the CIA *never* kidnaps children to raise for pet projects. Some of America's deep-cover spooks were born in foreign countries and moved here at young ages. Some had parents from foreign countries who taught them a first language other than English. Some learned a foreign language before the age of ten, and they were able to speak it without accent. Sometimes America gets lucky, and someone with just the right background, language skills, intelligence, and character chooses to dedicate themselves to the clandestine services, but no American operatives have ever been trained from birth for deep cover.

American deep-cover operatives train for various lengths of time and in different ways according to whether they are going into a country to be a bartender and listen or they are going into a country to hunt down enemies. Either way, a deep-cover assignment would virtually never last more than three years for an American.

The fact is that Americans generally like living in America. It's hard to get Americans to volunteer to live as locals in Russia, Communist China, Iran, or other hostile countries for more than a few years. They certainly don't want to marry, raise children, and grow old there. That was definitely true during the Cold War, as well. Few were willing to train for five years to live as Russians or Soviet Bloc residents. The flip side is that for spies from other countries, living in America is usually an upgrade, and they are happy for the task. It's a plum job.

We realize that sounds ethnocentric and perhaps a bit arrogant. That doesn't change the fact that it's easier for other countries to get their spies to come live here than it is for us to get our people to go live there. And there's one thing that's true above all else with spooks. Spooks deal in facts. They are hard-core realists about the world as it is, because you can't get to where you want to be tomorrow if you don't know where you stand today. It's just a fact.

Today, Russian operatives are able to come to America as Russians. They don't have to pretend to be Americans anymore. That's because at this point, Russians are not particularly rare, and many people know at least one person who has brought over a Russian mail-order bride. It's likely that Russia no longer invests in creating American towns in order to train its agents and slip them into our country. However, that can change with changing times.

The American IC does not know exactly how many Soviet sleeper agents were planted across the nation. We have no idea how many remained loyal and would have done their jobs. However, it is estimated that only 50 percent of them returned home with the dissolution of the Soviet Union.

We know what you're thinking about now . . . You're looking twice at that nice, elderly couple that runs the gas station near the interstate overpass. We're looking twice at them, too. #JustSaying

---

Bottom Line: The Soviet Union invested heavily in their sleeper agents and deep-cover agents and would not have used them for extensive active operations on American soil. The United States was never as successful at planting such operatives.

19

FIREARMS OF SPYCRAFT

SPYCRAFT INVOLVES BOTH HANDGUNS AND HIGHER-POWERED weapons. For those of you who are firearm aficionados, we appreciate your patience while we correct a few common misnomers and outright mistakes that we find throughout the fiction and nonfiction worlds. This chapter is not intended to be an exhaustive review of firearms, but rather a bit of focused, basic information for the purpose of eliminating some of the most common mistakes writers make.

There are basically three types of firearms used in spycraft—the revolver, the semiautomatic, and the automatic. When it comes to handguns, specifically, only revolvers and semiautomatics are commonly used by spooks, as the vast majority of automatics are rifles.

Contrary to popular belief, spooks use a variety of revolvers and semiautomatic handguns, and most of them are not made by Glock. In reality, though Glock has a stellar marketing department that seems to finagle the name "Glock" into almost every spook book, movie, and TV series made in the past twenty years, a spook will use whatever is most suited to them and to the job.

That could be a Glock, a Walther, a Smith & Wesson, a Beretta, a Makarov, or any other firearm that gives them an advantage of any kind for any reason.

Before we get to the differences in the types of handguns, though, we need to address two of the most common firearm misnomers of all time—the "bullet" vs. the "cartridge," and the "clip" vs. the "magazine."

BULLET vs. CARTRIDGE

A "cartridge" is the entirety of the brass, primer, gunpowder, and bullet that is loaded into a firearm. A "bullet" is the actual projectile that is fired from the end of a cartridge.

Image by Piper Bayard

On the left are 10mm hollow point bullets. On the right are 10mm hollow point cartridges. Note the bullet seated in the brass of the cartridge. The cartridge has a primer in the back end of the brass and contains gunpowder. The primer is the round component visible in the center of the back ends of the cartridges in the box on the right. When impacted, the primer ignites the gunpowder inside the cartridge. The force of the exploding gunpowder projects the bullet down the barrel and toward the target.

Writing Tip: Most of your readers won't know that the whole cartridge is not a "bullet," but that is no reason to continue perpetuating fiction in your . . . fiction. However, it is a writer's to serve the readers. Therefore, if preferred, the word "round" can be used in place of "cartridge" where the meaning of "cartridge" would not be understood. For example, "He loaded the cartridges into the revolver" is likely to be understood and is far more accurate than "loading bullets." However, if you doubt the sophistication of your readers, "He can load the 'rounds' into the revolver." A person can also put "rounds" into a target, indicating that the term is synonymous with "bullets" rather than "cartridges." It's a bit of a double standard to allow this flexibility with "round" but not with "bullet," but life is full of double standards. *Que sera, sera.*

CLIP vs. MAGAZINE

A magazine has a spring that force-feeds the ammo as the shooter fires. A clip has no spring or a feed mechanism. It simply holds the ammo and attaches to a magazine or inserts directly into a firearm.

Image by Piper Bayard

On the left half of the picture, we have an empty M1 Garand clip, an M1 Garand clip loaded with eight rounds of 30-06 ammunition, and the brass from a 30-06 spent cartridge. On the right half of the picture, we have nine rounds of 7.62x39 ammunition loaded onto a "stripper clip" and an empty stripper clip. This stripper clip holds ten rounds. The tenth 7.62x39 cartridge is just above the loaded clip. The clips are plain metal with no springs or gadgets of any kind that assist in feeding the ammunition through the firearm. Once the cartridges have been fired, the clips can be reloaded. However, in combat, that is highly unlikely. A clip would normally be discarded and a new clip loaded into the magazine or the magazine well, depending on the firearm.

Next we have "magazines." Magazines are widely used in both handguns and rifles. They can be detachable or not. They hold cartridges and can be quickly and easily reloaded. There are springs in the magazines that assist in feeding the ammunition through the firearms.

Image by Piper Bayard

The larger magazine is an "extended grip" 9mm SIG Sauer magazine, and the smaller magazine is from a Smith & Wesson Bodyguard .380. These magazines fit into the handles of the pistols.

Contrary to popular belief among certain circles of politicians who shall remain nameless, magazines are made of metal or plastic and can be reused countless times. They don't magically get "used up" just because all of the rounds are fired.

Time and time again in fiction, shooters reload their "clips" into their "automatic" pistols. Almost invariably, they are actually loading their "magazines" into "semiautomatics." Extremely few modern weapons being manufactured today use clips unless they are replicas of old weapons. One rare example of a modern weapon using a clip is the Smith & Wesson 9mm revolver, which uses a moon clip. So unless a character is using a historical weapon, or it is one of the rare modern firearms that take actual clips, the terminology is a fiction.

Writing Tip: If you're writing historical fiction, you might, indeed, have a weapon that uses a clip. If you are writing anything post-WWII, your weapon will likely have a magazine. We recommend you do a bit of research on the specific model of weapon in your manuscript, including the year it was made.

REVOLVERS

A revolver is so called because the cartridges reside in a revolving cylinder. Almost no revolver ever made has an actual manual safety mechanism. Like the semiautomatic, one trigger pull equals one shot. However, the brass shells are not ejected automatically. A shooter must open the cylinder and eject all of the shells simultaneously and reload. A shooter can hasten this process by using a "speed loader" to insert all of the cartridges with one motion. The legalities of revolver ownership vary from state to state, but revolvers are generally the most legally accepted of the varieties of handguns.

Things to remember about revolvers:

1. Ammunition is loaded into a cylinder.
2. Revolvers virtually never have manual safety mechanisms.
3. One trigger pull results in one shot.
4. No brass is ejected.
5. Legal in varying degrees according to state law.

Side Note: In some episodes of *The Walking Dead*, Rick fires his .357 Magnum Colt Python revolver, and you can hear the sound of the falling brass. Sound production fail. There is no falling brass from a revolver.

SEMIAUTOMATICS

With a semiautomatic, ammunition loads into a removable magazine that usually fits into the pistol grip. To reload, a shooter drops the empty magazine out of the grip and snaps in a full magazine. Most people are able to drop a magazine and snap a new one into a semiautomatic faster than they can reload a revolver; however, a skilled shooter is just as quick with a speed loader. Like the revolver, one trigger pull *always* equals one shot. *Unlike* the revolver, the brass is ejected with each shot.

Semiautomatics are legal in all states, but only to varying degrees in different places. In a few states, they practically come as prizes in the bottom of cereal boxes, while in others, only bodyguards of celebrities and politicians that advocate strict gun control get to carry them. In fact, if the celebrities and politicians are vocal enough in their opposition to private firearms, their bodyguards are approved to operate drones, drive tanks, and launch thermonuclear devices and other weapons of mass destruction.

It's extremely common for a semiautomatic to be inaccurately referred to throughout media, movies, and TV as an "automatic" weapon. No matter how hot the journalist, movie star, or soap opera star might be, don't believe it just because they say it.

"Bump stocks" gained notoriety after the mass shooting at a Country-Western music concert in Las Vegas in October, 2017. A bump stock is a type of stock that can be used on a semiautomatic rifle. The bump stock uses the recoil of the rifle to increase the rate at which a shooter can pull the trigger. In spite of what some politicians and Hollywood say, a bump stock does *not* create an "automatic weapon" out of a semiautomatic rifle, but with practice and skill, a bump stock can be used on a rifle to fire at the speed of an automatic weapon. Bump stocks are not used in any way in espionage or in the military. The Intelligence Community and the military do not bother with bump stocks because they have fully automatic weapons available to them.

Things to remember about the semiautomatic:

1. Ammunition is loaded in a magazine.
2. One trigger pull equals one shot.
3. Brass is ejected, usually to the right of the weapon, every time a shot goes off.
4. Legality varies according to state. Some states make semiautomatics difficult to obtain, or they restrict the size of the magazine. Other states have the Cracker Jack Box standard.

AUTOMATICS

With an automatic weapon, the cartridges load into a removable magazine. The weapon is called automatic because when a shooter pulls the trigger, it automatically fires repeated bullets until they take their finger off the trigger. When the shooter fires, the brass shells of the cartridges are ejected from the weapon at high speed.

Modern automatic weapons are generally illegal for private ownership without special government procedures—emphasis on "generally." There are three ways an individual in America can obtain an automatic weapon....

The Firearm Owners Protection Act of 1986 made it illegal for private individuals to acquire fully automatic weapons without special permission from the Bureau of Alcohol, Tobacco, and Firearms. Private gun owners can still obtain one of the pre-1986 fully automatic firearms if they fill out a form, wait several months, secure a tax stamp, and purchase the firearm for an exorbitant amount of money—exorbitant because, according to the National Rifle Association, there are only around 150,000 pre-1986 fully automatic weapons in private ownership.

The second way private individuals can obtain an automatic weapon is by going through the intense process of obtaining a license to manufacture Class III/NFA firearms. Once the individual has this license, they can secure a conversion kit to modify a semiautomatic rifle to make it fully automatic. With the hassle and expense, though, we recommend using the money for a nice beach vacation rather than pursuing one of these weapons.

The third way to obtain an automatic weapon in America is the timeless and ever-popular method known as theft. We do not recommend this method, especially with anyone who owns an automatic weapon. They might remember to use it on you.

Things to remember about automatics:

1. Ammunition is loaded in a magazine.
2. One trigger pull equals multiple shots.
3. Brass is ejected as the shooter is firing.

4. Illegal for private owners everywhere in the United States except with a very detailed, expensive process.

It's worth noting that different types of ammunition impact accuracy and are used for different purposes. For example, Bayard & Holmes use hollow points for self-defense because they are less likely to pass through the target and harm someone behind them. Different barrels with different types of rifling are also used depending on the purpose at hand. Firearms experts have written treatises about the many subtleties of ammunition and barrels. If you discuss types of ammunition and barrels in your fiction, we recommend you read one of these treatises before you commit your writing to stone or Kindle. If you make a mistake, firearms experts will call you on it, and they can be pretty rough about it.

Writing Tip: Be aware that no matter how much you research, there are firearms aficionados who will write to you about the rarest and most obscure exception to whatever you say and tell you you're stupid. Don't let that bother you. It's what they live for. Be reasonably diligent in your vocabulary, hit the big things like "revolver," "semiautomatic," "automatic," "clip," "magazine," "bullet," and "cartridge," and you can be pretty sure the vast majority of your readers will be satisfied. As for the rest, don't feed the trolls.

MISCELLANEOUS GUN FACTS

1. Gun at the forehead

Over and over in fiction, we see both the bad guys and the good guys shoving their pistols right up against people, either into their sides or at their foreheads. That's a great technique if a shooter never wants a second shot.

In real life, the pressure of firing a pistol with the barrel right up against a barrier can ruin the weapon and prevent the shooter from ever getting off another shot. For best results, shooters should hold their firearms an inch from the target. The target still gets the point, and if the spook has to shoot them, it won't ruin their pistol.

2. Running with Guns

We can look in almost any thriller and see people running with pistols and rifles in their hands. In real life, even a small pistol in the hand can throw a runner slightly off balance and slow them down. A spook will always prefer to holster a weapon while they are running if it is at all feasible.

3. Ammo in a Skillet

In the movie *RED*, which we thoroughly enjoyed, Bruce Willis places cartridges in a skillet and heats them on the stove. When they reach a certain temperature, they begin firing off bullets at high speed in a variety of directions. It's a beautiful concept, and it makes for a very fun scene, but it's pure fiction.

In real life, when cartridges are heated, they will indeed pop open, but without the barrel of a gun to direct the energy, the bullets won't be propelled very far in one direction. It's the barrel of a pistol directing that explosive energy that allows for a bullet to travel far and fast. It's not the cartridge or the gunpowder alone.

4. Speed of Bullets

In *The November Man*, which is a tribute to espionage myths, Pierce Brosnan's character explains that a bullet from a pistol will be traveling at four times the speed of sound. All we can say is that Hollywood is once again holding out on the US military.

The world's fastest commercially-produced pistol at the time of publication, according to the National Rifle Association, is the 7.5 FK Brno, which can propel bullets at a speed of 2000 fps, just under two times the sound barrier. The top speed of most modern commercially available rifle cartridges is right around three times the speed of sound, and the fastest commercial rifle cartridge in the world at the time of publication is the .220 Swift, which barely breaks four times the speed of sound.

This is only one example of the many spook myths in *The November Man*. We ask that if you see the movie, you please don't believe one bit of it.

5. Ian Fleming's Favorite Weapon

One might think from the Bond series that it would be the Walther PPK. However, Fleming's favorite weapon was a Smith & Wesson, which was presented to him by General William "Wild Bill" Donovan.

6. Spooks call them guns.

There is the popular fiction in fiction that "real" spooks and agents never call a pistol or rifle a "gun," but instead always call them a "pistol," "rifle," "firearm," "piece," "heater," "widowmaker," and anything else except a "gun." In real life, spooks often use the word "gun" to refer to their . . . guns. It's such a widespread idea in the publishing world, though, that we actually adjust our characters' dialogue in our fiction to conform so that our fellow writers don't write us off out of hand. Spooks, however, never give the word a second thought.

20

SILENCERS

FOR SIMPLICITY'S SAKE, WE WILL USE THE TERMS "SUPPRESSOR" AND "silencer" interchangeably in this chapter.

Movies and books would convince us that any firearm can be silenced down to a tiny *pfftzing* sound when fired. Not so!

The purpose of silencers for spooks is to keep anyone from recognizing the sound of a gunshot and screaming, calling 911, or returning fire. In most cases, the spook doesn't care if someone hears the shot as long as they don't recognize it as a shot. People will normally ignore noises that they hear but don't associate with gunshots or other dangers. Because of this human tendency, the level of "silencing" characters need with their firearms will depend on their situations.

For example, if a spook intends to walk into a steel mill and shoot someone, they don't need much. On the other hand, if they want to shoot someone in a library without being noticed, they had better have a high degree of silencing.

Ever wonder why Bond always uses the Walther PPK .380 in the field? It's not just because it's cute and German. It's because the

.380 semiautomatic provides enough energy for close-up assassination while still being capable of effective and inexpensive silencing.

In fact, the only more powerful mass-produced auto-loading weapon that *can* be efficiently and cheaply silenced is the Russian knockoff of the Walther PPK, the Makarov .380, which is like a regular .380 on steroids. With a bullet slightly wider and heavier than that of the standard .380, the Makarov has the maximum energy of any *subsonic* cartridge that the Soviet firearms specialists could put into a straight blowback semiautomatic design.

THE SONIC BOOM

The term "subsonic" is important when discussing silencers or suppressors because a bullet traveling faster than the speed of sound makes a sonic boom that cannot be silenced. Simply put, the subsonic cartridges are much quieter and, therefore, more practical for silenced firearms.

THE SLIDE MECHANISM

The .380 can be silenced because it is small enough to have a straight blowback design, while larger handguns have the delayed blowback design. The blowback design refers to how the slide operates when the pistol cycles ammunition. With the straight blowback design, the pistol can be modified to *manually lock the slide in a closed position* so the weapon can fire without causing the cartridges to jam. The locked slide prevents the noise of the slide operation along with the sound that escapes the ejection port when the pistol cycles. *The noise of the slide cannot be silenced except by locking it in place.* When a "locked" pistol is used with a cylindrical suppressor threaded onto its muzzle, the combination allows for the highest level of sound suppression.

Unlike the movies, to fire successive shots in real life, a shooter of a silenced pistol must manually unlock the slide, cycle out the cartridge, and then relock the slide before taking a second shot. Locking and unlocking is accomplished with a small lever that would resemble the safety lever on a slide. With a bit of practice, it can be operated in approximately one second without much effort.

While a pistol with a manual slide lock does not allow for the quickest successive shots, it can be very quiet, making it ideal for some situations. For example, if the shooter intends to assassinate an individual who is walking home on his usual route after work, he could easily get a close-up head shot on a side street. The noise would be low enough that someone walking twenty yards ahead of the victim would not notice it. Another example is if the shooter can gain access to the target when the target is alone in his hotel room, home, or office. In such circumstances, a trained shooter can easily take the time to deliver a second "insurance" shot on a high-value target without a hotel maid in the hallway or people in the next room hearing anything.

Writing Tip: One danger to silencing properly with a handgun is that the shooter will forget to lock the slide after cycling in the second round. The weapon will still be suppressed, but it will still make more noise than it would if the slide were locked. If you need a character to make a mistake while firing with a silencer, this is a logical one.

A .380 without a manual slide lock installed is also popular to use with a modern liquid-filled suppressor. Such a weapon would make more noise than a locked Makarov or .380, but it would still be quieter than a .22 short cartridge fired from a .22 rifle. Spooks might use this if they are alone with the target inside a closed hotel room, office, home, etc., and the noise level would still be acceptable. In other words, a pedestrian twenty yards away on a quiet street might recognize the sound as a gunshot, but a pedestrian standing or walking around the corner of a city block would not notice the sound of this type of suppressed weapon.

THE FALLING BRASS

The sound of falling brass is also impossible to silence. Only spooks in movies don't have to worry about that ping. To prevent the brass from falling, spooks can carry specially designed brass catchers that they can attach to the pistols. However, the act of attaching them can slow down a shooter. Also, the catcher, itself, is one more piece of evidence that can be found on a spook, and less evidence is always better.

A more down-and-dirty trick, so to speak, is to use a sock as a brass catcher. Holmes doesn't like this method, though, because it blows out the end of the sock, which could lead to the brass falling anyway. Also, the sock could catch in the slide and jam it. And, again, it leaves one more piece of evidence. So as a general rule, most spooks risk the sound of falling brass.

We know what you're thinking . . . But, wait! If a spook doesn't have a brass catcher, isn't the brass evidence?

Not so much as one might think. That's because an intelligent, professional spook uses "clean brass." Clean brass is brass that would not be identified as American brass, and it would have no fingerprints. Spooks don't have to worry about leaving it behind.

WHAT ABOUT SILENCING REVOLVERS?

During the 1970s, one of the most popular handguns in movies was the attractive Colt Python .357 Magnum revolver. We often saw scenes with "silenced" Pythons being fired with a mild *pfftz* sound. The revolver mechanics somehow made no noise at all. Magically, the gas that escaped from between the cylinder and the barrel made no noise, either. That only happens in movies. *Suppressors* can be used on revolvers, but with much less effect than can be achieved with an auto-loading pistol with a locked slide.

Currently, the most popular suppressed handguns in the movies are the 9mm autoloader and the .45 ACP autoloader. With modern suppressors, they can be partially silenced. With precision machining and greater expense, larger handguns can be suppressed, but not to the same degree as the .380 or the .380 Makarov.

When a shooter doesn't want to wake up people in a neighboring apartment or alert police on the next block, those weapons are effective, but unlike in the movies, a guard standing ten yards away is definitely going to notice the sound of the pistol—not to mention the sound of the falling body. Nonetheless, if a shooter ever had to fire an *unsuppressed* 9mm or similar pistol from inside of a car, his first thought would be, "Ouch, my ears *really* hurt." His second thought would be, "I wish I had a suppressor on this thing."

Another popular "silenced" weapon is the Hollywood High-Power Sniper Rifle. It can be fired accurately from any distance with only a slight *pfftz* sound, there is no crack when the bullet breaks the sound barrier, and the shooter never runs out of ammo. Unfortunately for the US military, Hollywood is holding out, and it isn't sharing any of those fine weapons.

In real life, a suppressor can partially reduce the noise made by a high-powered rifle, and it can distort perception of the precise origin of the shot. However, as long as that rifle is firing a supersonic bullet, it's not going to be anything like "quiet." Less noisy? Yes. Unnoticed downrange? Not likely. The only advantage in suppressing a high-power rifle that fires supersonic bullets is that the shots would alert people over a smaller radius than if a suppressor were not used.

But there's good news for Hollywood and for snipers.

In recent years, high-power cartridges have been developed to fire heavier bullets at subsonic velocities. One example would be the .300 Whisper. These cartridges lack the flatter trajectories of supersonic bullets, but they also lack the loud sonic "crack" generated by supersonic bullets.

THE FALLING BODY

The sound of a falling body is a third thing that cannot be silenced. Dead bodies drop, and they aren't always conveniently located in an open space with a thick carpet. They can smash into furniture and knock things over. They can break glass and thump into floors and walls. If in a bathroom and the body falls against a cast-iron tub, it makes a loud, heavy ringing sound. Catching a body to prevent the noise of the fall poses the equally risky problem of the spook being covered in blood. Bloody people tend to have trouble blending in when walking out of a building or down a street. It's just an inconvenient truth that bodies fall where they die, and the possibilities are infinite.

> **Bottom Line:** Three things cannot be silenced—the shells being ejected, the crack of the sound barrier, and a falling body. Which brings us to the fourth thing that cannot be silenced—the savvy reader who sends a writer angry e-mails if they get this wrong.

Writing Tip: One man's inconvenient truth is another man's plotline. Feel free to have fun with falling bodies. You're not likely to take it too far.

Side Note: Not all bullets stop in the first body they reach. Many pass through, depending on the caliber of the weapon and the ammunition used. A bullet can quite feasibly go through the target and out a window and kill a little old lady or her Pomeranian.

21

WHERE TO SHOOT THE TARGET

WHERE A SHOOTER AIMS ON A TARGET DEPENDS ON THE WEAPON they are using and whether their ultimate goal is to capture or to kill.

LONG-RANGE SNIPING

A sniper will aim for the head or for the heart, depending on the circumstances. Those circumstances include theweather, the reason the operative is sniping, who he's sniping, distance, angle, view, whether target is moving or still, and limitless other factors. As a *general* rule, as long as the sniper is using at least a .308 sniper rifle, like the US Marine Corps M40, with the proper modern ammunition within eight hundred meters, any hit on torso, head, or hips will likely be fatal.

Death with a chest or head shot occurs within milliseconds. A hip shot will disable the target within seconds and, without immediate help from a competent medic, will kill the target within two to four minutes due to the bullet fragmenting into the lower torso, internal bleeding, and shock from the intense pain. Even with a competent medic, death is likely.

CLOSE-RANGE PISTOL

As a general rule, most shooters are in the habit of aiming "center mass," or at the torso. For that reason, if a spook is in the same room with the target, most will choose to go with a "double tap," which is two shots to the chest, followed by a head shot. If a target is wearing a protective vest, though, a shooter must go for the head or the hip. If a shooter hits the target's hip, the target will usually fall down backward. At that point, the smart spook will put a second round up through the groin as the target is going down.

Why shoot again if the target is down? Because even if the target is down, they can shoot back before they die. If field spooks are going to survive to complete the mission, they must leave questions of how much force was "enough" to the ivory towers and the safe bubbles of courtrooms. In the real world, a spook must worry about whether or not five more attackers are behind the first one. With multiple targets or the potential of multiple targets, a spook can't waste a great deal of time on the first one. Also, if the shot person lives, they could blow the spook's cover. Decisions must be made in a heartbeat, and often, a spook's survival depends on their skill at rapidly evaluating a situation and making those decisions.

SHOOTING TO CAPTURE vs. SHOOTING TO KILL

Sometimes, it is more advantageous to capture a target than it is to kill them. It could be the target has information, or they might be someone that could be traded for something of value to the spook. In some such cases, for example during a raid or some other kinetic event, it may be expedient for the spook to shoot the person to capture them. Under such circumstances, the spook is best off going for a shot to the person's arm rather than a leg or torso.

The arm shot takes more skill than a leg or torso, but it has two advantages for a capture. First, a target is less likely to bleed out from an arm shot. If a spook shoots a target in the calf and the shot is a little too high, the target could bleed out and die too soon. It doesn't do much good to capture a target if they die before a spook can get them to an appropriate location for interrogation. And second, if the target is shot in the arm, they can still walk. A spook might need them to march through a jungle or over a mountain to get them somewhere for questioning. When crossing such terrain, it's much easier for a spook to get where they are going if they don't have to carry someone else who doesn't want to be there.

Bottom Line: If a spook needs a target dead, they don't mess around. If a spook needs a target alive, an arm shot is best. No one wants to climb a mountain for two.

22

COVERT COMMUNICATIONS

SPOOKS OFTEN COMMUNICATE WITH EACH OTHER USING ENCRYPTED messages via the Internet or radio signals. This may include satellite systems or shortwave, long-distance radio messages or even encrypted phone systems. Within the United States, it's fairly safe for spooks to use these phones and computers.

The problem, however, with phones and computers is that they can be hacked. As noted above, even the Pentagon gets hacked. So spooks also communicate by meeting each other in person at a restaurant, a park, a remote location, or anywhere else they can speak without being near windows or curious ears. And, of course, there are the age-old standbys known as dead drops and brush passes.

TRADITIONAL DEAD DROPS

Dead drops are unmanned locations where spooks, agents, and cutouts can exchange cash, information, or other articles without physically meeting or being in the same place at the same time. That way, even if one of the parties is caught, the enemy doesn't necessarily catch both.

A dead drop could be in a park or a deserted area. For example, it could be in a hollowed-out tree or under a rock near a rural road. Or, if you're the CIA, it's a fake rock or brick with a compartment inside that can be set by the roadside or on a pile in a construction area. However, a spook knows they are screwed if they drive up and see a bunch of teenagers flinging bricks against a wall, so it has to be left in an out-of-the-way location where the spook can reasonably expect that a passerby won't pick it up. Another CIA favorite used from the 1960s through the 1990s was a hollow spike, much like a fat tent stake, that was pushed into the ground at a prearranged location. Generally, a dead drop can be any unremarkable-looking container or natural feature in a low-traveled area.

Once a spook places something in a dead drop, they leave a discreet signal somewhere, such as a mark on a tree, curb, or mailbox to indicate that the person or group they are communicating with needs to check the dead drop. This can be any prearranged, agreed-to mark that can be seen by someone walking or driving by. The mark just needs to be something that blends in and that no one would notice if they weren't looking for it. For example, during the Cold War, it was common for the Soviets to use chalk marks on post office boxes to indicate that a dead drop needed to be checked. (The final season of *The Americans* has great examples of this trick.) In fact, this practice was so common that US postmen were trained to watch for chalk marks.

Robert Hanssen

One infamous employer of dead drops in the United States was US traitor Robert Hanssen. Robert Hanssen was a husband, a father of six, a devout Catholic, and a member of Opus Dei, a conservative Catholic fraternity. He was also an FBI agent who sold information to the Soviet Union and Russia for twenty years.

Hanssen held key counterintelligence positions and was stationed in both New York and Washington, DC. During over twenty separate occasions, he passed the Soviet KGB and later the Russian SVR over two dozen computer diskettes and over six thousand pages of classified documents. He also compromised numerous human resources, including betraying Dmitri Polyakov,* a CIA informant who rose to the rank of general in the Soviet Army. In return, Hanssen received over six hundred thousand dollars from the Soviets.

The FBI arrested Hanssen on February 18, 2001, at his favorite Foxstone Park dead drop, code named "Ellis," near his home in Vienna, Virginia. He is still rotting, preferably miserably, in the ADX Florence supermax prison near Florence, Colorado, serving out fifteen consecutive life sentences. He spends twenty-three hours each day in solitary confinement. We here at Bayard & Holmes, in a gesture of compassion, are starting a GoFundMe site to hire prison guards for Robbie that were trained at the Soviet Vorkuta Gulag so he can be surrounded by the people to whom he sold out his country. Robert Hanssen is widely considered to be the most damaging spy in the history of the FBI.

Learn more about Robert Hanssen in our upcoming release, *Key Figures in Espionage: The Good, the Bad, and the Booty*.

*The Soviets did not arrest Polyakov until after he was betrayed a second time by CIA operative and Soviet spy Aldrich Ames in 1985. The Soviets executed Polyakov in 1988 by shooting him in a small walled courtyard inside the Kremlin. That's the Kremlin for you. One-stop shopping.

DIGITAL DEAD DROPS

Even hacker group Anonymous hasn't figured out yet how to hack a piece of paper. However, in this digital age, it is possible to imagine digital dead drops. We encourage you to use your imaginations. And that is all we will say about that.

BRUSH PASS

A brush pass is the opposite of a dead drop, as it is an actual exchange of cash, information, or other articles directly between two people. This method of exchange is usually only used when a matter is urgent, forcing the participants to rush things. It's not the preferred method of communication because if one person is successfully tailed, both could be caught, along with their valuables and any incriminating evidence.

While dead drops are off the beaten path, a brush pass takes place in a train station at rush hour, on a busy street, or at least by ducking into opposite ends of a building to meet in a bathroom. Without stopping and talking or making eye contact, the two parties brush past each other, and something gets exchanged.

A controller, or "handler," is an operative that "runs" foreign agents. Usually the handler will not conduct a brush pass but instead will send an unknown individual, as in someone less likely to be known by anyone who might be tailing that operative. The agent they are meeting will only know to look for "a woman in a plaid skirt and jacket with red hair" or some other identifiable feature.

If the handler needs to meet directly with the agent, they will usually send someone to meet the agent and then take them somewhere else, making sure to shake any possible watchers along the way. Some ways the person transporting the agent might do this would be to drive to a mall, walk in the south side, walk out the north side, and get in a different car to drive off. They might go in a building and then either exit the opposite end of the building or have a double come back out the same door. They might have the agent disguised in a hoodie and sunglasses going into the building and have a double dressed exactly the same way exiting a different door while the agent removes the hoodie and sunglasses and exits a third door to a waiting vehicle. The possibilities are endless if they are kept within the framework of setting and circumstances.

> **Writing Tip:** As we mentioned in the Fifty Shades of "Covert" chapter earlier, when a spook is shaking a tail, it's the time to pull out all the drama. See how creative you can be within the framework of reality, your setting, and your characters. You won't get any criticism from us, and we might even borrow your ideas for real life.

23

POISONS

WESTERN INTELLIGENCE ORGANIZATIONS RARELY USE POISON TO kill, and the garden variety Western field operative doesn't know much about them. This is for two basic reasons. First, assassinations are rare in the West. There simply isn't much occasion to use poisons. And second, in the rare occurrence of an assassination, poison is almost as practical and efficient as chaining Bond above a shark tank.

For a spook to deliver the poison without risking killing random people other than the target, they must get right next to either the target or their food. Someone who needs a good killing, such as an Idi Amin or a Moammar Gadhafi, has food testers and closely monitored cooks. In the incredibly rare event that an assassination is sanctioned and even rarer occasion that a spook would be using poison to kill a target, the spook would receive specific training about the poison for that assignment and possibly an antidote to the poison or a regimen to build up tolerance to it.

It is slightly more common for spooks in the West to use a nonfatal poison as part of a "snatch job," or kidnapping. In that instance, a spook might use a poison to incapacitate someone so they had to leave their workplace and go to a doctor or a hospital. That's because it's easier to snatch someone when they are away from their normal locations. However, even nonfatal poisonings would be very rare events for Western spooks.

Soviets/Russians are much fonder of poisons than are spooks in the West. It's not just due to their dramatic nature, but to the fact that, as a general rule, Russians couldn't care less about collateral damage, as in killing innocents, whether in the espionage field or the military arena. One great example of this was the 2006 assassination of Alexander Litvinenko.

ALEXANDER LITVINENKO

Litvinenko was a Russia FSB officer who specialized in taking down organized crime. In 1998, he and several of his fellow officers accused their FSB superiors of having ordered the assassination of Boris Berezovsky, a Russian oligarch. Rather than assassinate Berezovsky, Litvinenko warned him, which Berezovsky said later he believed saved his life. Litvinenko was then arrested and released twice on charges of exceeding his authority. In 2000, after the second time the charges were dismissed, Litvinenko escaped with his family to the United Kingdom.

In London, Litvinenko worked as a paid consultant for MI6 on Russian organized crime. He was also a journalist and an author, penning two books, *Blowing Up Russia: Terror from Within* and *Lubyanka Criminal Group,* in which he accused the Russian secret services of staging terrorist attacks to help bring Vladimir Putin to power. Litvinenko was also certain that Putin ordered the 2006 murder of Russian journalist Anna Politkovskaya, and that Putin is a pedophile. Litvinenko was the first to apply the term "Mafia state" to Putin's Russia, meaning a state in which the roles of government, organized crime, and espionage agencies are merged and have become indistinguishable.

In the fall of 2006, Litvinenko was set to testify before a Spanish prosecutor that Russian Mafia connections in Spain went as far back as the 1990s and that numerous senior Russian officials were complicit. His testimony would have directly implicated Putin, who was president of Russia at that time. Russia sent two assassins, Andrei Lugovoi and Dmitry Kovtun, along with the rare radioactive isotope polonium-210 to London to stop Litvinenko before he could testify.

Once in London, Lugovoi and Kovtun's first attempt on Litvinenko's life was to poison his glass of water at a business meeting. Litvinenko, likely cagey after pissing off so many unscrupulous Russians, did not drink from his glass that day.

After that, Lugovoi brought his unsuspecting family in for the next assassination attempt—his wife; his two daughters; his eight-year-old son, Igor; a daughter's boyfriend; and an old family friend. The entire group checked into the Millennium Hotel under the pretense of being in London for a soccer game. The next day, cameras at the hotel show Lugovoi going into the men's room and coming out. An hour later, Kovtun arrived at the hotel and did the same. There were no cameras in the men's room to know what they did in there, but investigators later discovered extreme alpha radiation contamination in a bathroom stall and underneath the hand dryer. Some readings were so high that they were off the scale.

Lugovoi and Litvinenko were familiar with each other, as both had been part of Boris Berezovsky's entourage in the 1990s. Lugovoi had recontacted Litvinenko in 2005 to discuss working together as consultants advising Western firms wanting to invest in Russia. On November 1, 2006, Lugovoi invited Litvinenko to meet him in the Pine Bar of the Millennium Hotel. The assassin encouraged Litvinenko to "hurry up" because Lugovoi wanted to see the soccer game.

When Litvinenko arrived, several cups and a teapot were already set at the table. The waiter asked if Litvinenko wanted to order anything, and Lugovoi indicated that Litvinenko was welcome to drink from the pot of tea he had already ordered. Litvinenko did so. Twenty-three days later, he died in the hospital, the first confirmed case of polonium-210-induced acute radiation syndrome. However, Litvinenko did not die before recording extensive testimony about his own murder, placing the blame squarely on Putin.

Forensic investigators found high levels of radioactive contamination at the table and in the teapot that was used that day. Before the source of the poisoning was discovered, the Millennium Hotel had continued to serve people tea in the contaminated teapot and washed it in the dishwasher with spoons, cups, plates, etc. People continued to use the contaminated men's room, and people continued to stay in the guest room where Dmitry Kovtun poured the remainder of the polonium-210 down the sink. There is no knowing how many people received life-shortening exposure to radiation during the course of the assassination. We do know the name of one, however. Winning the Extreme Parent Fail competition, Lugovoi made it a point to return to the Pine Bar with his son, Igor, where Lugovoi instructed the boy to shake hands with the now-contaminated Litvinenko.

This type of depraved indifference to innocents is classic Russian style. However, the Litvinenko assassination exemplifies why poisons are difficult to deliver, and many are difficult to contain— exactly the reason governments in the West rarely use them. It is also an illustration of the truth of what DEA Agent Steve Murphy says in the Netflix Original Series *Narcos*. "You want to call me a bad guy? Fine. But if you do, it just means you haven't met enough bad guys yet to know the difference."

More recently, in March of 2018, the Russians allegedly attempted to assassinate former Russian GRU intelligence officer Sergei Skripal with the nerve agent novichok. Both he and his daughter were found comatose on a bench outside a shopping center in Salisbury, UK. They, along with nineteen other exposed people, received medical attention. After weeks in comas, both Skripals survived. At the time of publication, the Skripals had relocated within the UK and were keeping their location a secret. The investigation is ongoing.

The Soviets/Russians don't just rely on the sort of indiscriminate poisoning demonstrated in the Litvinenko assassination. They also get into cute, Bond-esque delivery methods. One of the Soviet's most famous Bond-esque poisonings was the 1978 assassination of Georgi Markov, a Bulgarian dissident writer who had worked for the Bulgarian intelligence service. Markov escaped to the West and worked as a broadcaster and journalist for the BBC and Radio Free Europe. The Soviets assassinated him in London by delivering a ricin pellet on the tip of an umbrella. Markov died four days later.

Another classic that the KGB was known for was the gold cigarette case that functioned as a pellet gun, delivering a pellet of powerful toxin at close range. The West first became aware of this weapon in 1954 when the Soviets sent one of their spies, Nikolai Khokhlov, to Frankfurt to assassinate an anticommunist leader. When Khokhlov arrived in Frankfurt, he instead defected to the United States. His equipment included a gold cigarette case that was made to fire small cyanide-tipped pellets. The Soviets used this weapon during the late 1950s and early 1960s, and it is believed the KGB employed it repeatedly over time to kill off people at the United Nations.

Bottom Line: Poisons are not commonly used in the West. They are more commonly used by governments such as Russia, which aren't so picky about who they take down with their target.

Writing Tip: Feel free to explore the boundaries of your imagination when it comes to poisons, but keep in mind that they are not used widely by ethical spooks.

24

WEAPONIZED GADGETS

WEAPONIZED GADGETS WERE AND ARE ALSO USED AS FIREARMS. KGB officer Bogdan Stashynsky, who assassinated Ukrainian nationalist leaders Lev Rebet and Stepan Bandera before defecting to the West in 1961, was known for using a gas-powered gun rolled up in a newspaper. The Soviets also had a one-shot lipstick pistol that they used during the sixties. As for the West, the British had the smoking gun—a smoking pipe gun, that is. It looked like Grandpa's pipe and delivered a small projectile to kill at close range. Proof that smoking kills. . . . Sorry. We couldn't help ourselves.

We could go on, but the International Spy Museum does it better. Check out these and other clever spy gadgets at their web site, International Spy Museum at https://www.spymuseum.org.

Bottom Line: When it comes to weaponized gadgets for delivering either poison or a projectile, the only limit is imagination.

Writing Tip: If you need your character to have a weaponized gadget or a gadget rigged for surveillance, look around your office or in your purse and choose an object that won't draw attention. Just make sure it's large enough to deliver a poison or a projectile strong enough to kill. If your character is Russian, feel free to kill as many bystanders as necessary to get the job done. It's what they would do.

25
TRUTH SERUMS AND ENHANCED INTERROGATIONS

ENHANCED INTERROGATIONS HAVE ALWAYS BEEN AN UNPLEASANT, but sometimes necessary, part of information gathering. This has been true since Ogg's tribe captured a scout from rival Grub's tribe and had a chat about Grub's territorial ambitions regarding future mammoth hunts. More than once throughout history, interrogators have wished for a "truth serum" they could force down Grub's throat during these interrogations that would get him to cough up reliable information. Over the past decades, scientists, the military, intelligence organizations, police, prosecutors, and parents of wayward teenagers have looked hopefully to modern chemistry and medicine to produce such a silver bullet. Sadly, best efforts have been, at best, disappointing.

> *"It's safe to assume every intelligence organization and every prosecutor in the world wishes there were an effective truth serum."* ~ Jay Holmes

"Truth serums" are pretty iffy business, and to an extent, they all depend on the person being questioned. The Soviets were always bigger on their use and development than the United States ever was, but we are not aware of any great successes the Soviets may have had with them, either. At this point in time, interrogations must hang on other techniques.

Though all spooks get some basic training in interrogation, it is actually a specialty that requires advanced training and a particular personality. A good interrogator is quick-minded, a good listener, and patient, and they are skilled at knowing just how far they can go with various methods.

When we say "various methods," we aren't talking about pulling out people's fingernails or blinding them with an ice pick. We largely aren't talking about torture at all. That's why it's called "enhanced interrogations" and not "torture sessions." As a general rule, subtler forms of interrogation are more effective than torture when a spook needs information. That's because in most cases, a person being tortured will say whatever it takes to make the pain stop. Sure, information comes fast, but it's not necessarily reliable information.

Sleep deprivation, for example, is often a better method of obtaining information if a spook has the time for it. Over a period of days, an interrogator can piece together information and discover contradictions. However, when sleep deprivation is carried too far, it can be counterproductive. People will start babbling and admitting to anything. A good interrogator knows just how far to push this and other methods.

Isolation is another good tool for interrogations with some people because it helps break down a person's resistance. For many people, when their identity and beliefs are not being reinforced by external influences, they stop caring. Once they stop caring, a good interrogator can get to the heart of the matter. To a true psychopath, however, isolation won't have much effect because they are always isolated in their own heads already.

WATERBOARDING

Some people think the post-9/11 waterboarding scandal was some sort of watershed event. If the media is to be believed, waterboarding was discovered by investigative reporters, and for the first time in history, the US Congress became aware of physical torture. In its narrative, Congress stepped in to stop the practice of waterboarding and bring that naughty CIA to heel. Nothing could be further from the truth. (Refer to The Life Cycle of Controversial Practices mentioned earlier.) After a great deal of media hype, which generated a great deal of financial profits for news outlets, President Obama banned waterboarding in 2008. Waterboarding was a useful technique, but it was not a perfect technique, and there is no agreement within the Intelligence Community as to how this change has impacted the effectiveness of interrogations.

However, the thing the IC does agree on is that there is no golden bullet when it comes to interrogation. Neither waterboarding nor any other method is a sure thing. Ultimately, the effectiveness of any interrogation method comes down to the skill and experience of the interrogators.

Side Note: Some European allies that are most vocal in criticizing the United States for torture have no hesitation in using it on their own prisoners.

Bottom Line: Torture is, in our opinion, not as profitable as subtler methods of enhanced interrogation if there is time to use those subtler methods, and America is not the torture capital that popular antimilitary, anti-intelligence culture makes it out to be.

Writing Tip: If you're writing American spooks, don't make them eager to stab out people's eyes or cut off their balls to get them to talk. Some pain is realistic in a field interrogation, but too much pain, and people will say anything. That's not helpful, so be creative. As for Third World characters or Mafiosi, a fast track to extreme measures is sadly realistic.

26

CENTRAL AMERICA AND THE SCHOOL OF THE AMERICAS

FREQUENTLY WHEN PEOPLE THINK OF ENHANCED INTERROGATIONS or torture, they harken back to the Cold War, when the US was involved in keeping the Soviet Union from solidifying its influence in Central America. There is a myth in the media and in popular culture that the US Army and the CIA went to Central America during the Cold War to teach hitherto peace-loving Central Americans in Utopia how to use violence. In reality, Central American police, military personnel, and politicians were well versed and exceedingly ruthless in the use of indiscriminate brutality.

Central American police, military personnel, and politicians often committed assassinations and were known to slaughter entire villages if they thought anyone in those villages had assisted any communist guerillas. A few of those massacres are well documented, such as the slaughter of an estimated eight hundred civilians at El Mozote in El Salvador in December 1981. El Mozote is still considered the worst massacre in modern Central American history.

In addition to the government forces working against Soviet- and Cuban-backed communist incursions, there were the numerous death squads that came and went. In order to understand what these death squads were and where they came from, we want to pause a moment and emphasize a fact of world affairs that Americans and other Westerners rarely consider or understand.

Countries like the United States, the United Kingdom, Canada, Australia, New Zealand, and their ilk are orderly countries. Their presidents, prime ministers, parliament, etc., make laws and direct their intelligence, military, and executive branches. Military leaders might disagree, but they value the civil system and comply. Likewise, intelligence leaders, state and district leaders, city and town leaders, and ordinary citizens might grumble amongst themselves about the top executive and the legislative bodies being full of self-serving crooks whose shoe sizes outstrip their IQs, but for the sake of civil order, they largely comply. The US president doesn't need to worry about the Secret Service plotting his assassination. The UK prime minister doesn't need to worry about her military generals staging a coup. The Canadian prime minister doesn't need to worry about his intelligence personnel working with foreign operatives to undermine his operations abroad. Sadly, such cohesive governments are the exception on the planet rather than the rule.

This was particularly true in Central America during the Cold War. Assassinations and executions were not just common, they were expected. As one of Piper's law school professors explained, he was in Costa Rica at a high-end cocktail party when Nixon's resignation was announced. The suited gentleman he was chatting with matter-of-factly asked, "When will Mr. Nixon be executed?" It is a cultural blind spot for Americans to think that other people, other cultures, and other governments are just like ours, with the same social goals and values. They are not. The death squads of Central America are perhaps one of the greatest examples of this diversity.

DEATH SQUADS

The perception in media and in popular culture is that death squads are a single, centrally organized entity. They are not and never have been.

"Death squad" is the name given to pretty much any group with weapons and ammo that goes around killing people, and in Central America, they predate the American Revolution. During the Cold War, automatic weapons were ubiquitous, and it was a rare upper-middle-class or upper-class family that didn't have a stash of weapons and ammo. Plenty of poor people had them, as well, having picked them up from dead or defecting government soldiers or leftists. With this kind of supply, people banded their relatives and allies together into death squads on any given day for pretty much any reason—because they had a land dispute with their neighbor, because they wanted to run an electrical line across a road, because Juan's son winked at Guillermo's daughter, etc. Many of these squads claimed right-wing politics. Some claimed left-wing politics. Many were not at all political, though they often used politics as the public excuse for their actions.

The popular Cold War Central American myth, versus the actual history, is that the CIA got the "novel idea" of giving locals guns and telling them to kill each other, thus forming the Central American death squads. That is purely a fantasy of affluent American thinking fueled by lazy journalism. While the CIA certainly had a presence in Central America during the Cold War, it had no use for wild-ass local death squads that killed indiscriminately and couldn't keep their mouths shut. If the CIA needed to kill someone in the fight against the Soviets, they had plenty of loyal, proficient Americans on hand to do the job.

The death squads were, in fact, counterproductive to the CIA's counterterrorism goals and to the interests of the United States. The locals would slaughter entire villages and torture prisoners in ways that would curl even George R. R. Martin's toes. The fear and chaos only contributed to the tumultuous atmosphere that was opening the door ever wider to the communists.

The Soviets were eager to gain footholds in the Western Hemisphere, and this savage behavior on the part of Central American governments created fertile ground for Soviet-backed communist agents to recruit locals. As a result, every US Army Special Forces officer and every CIA operative who served in Central America during that time dreamed of convincing the Central American governments to be less ruthless with their own citizens.

The idea that the CIA was employing locals in death squads was largely born of the imagination of lazy journalists. US journalists were delighted to do those tell-all interviews with the "participants" and/or "firsthand witnesses" of violence and assassinations. While no doubt there were *some* honest journalists in Central America, the vast majority of journalists never actually went closer to a jungle than a bar in Tegucigalpa or San Salvador, and the only interviews they conducted were with "firsthand witnesses" and with their fellow journalists, making up the crap they thought their readers might want to hear.

THE WITNESSING INDUSTRY

Notice we put "firsthand witnesses" in quotation marks....

"Professional witnessing was a cottage industry. Having actually witnessed anything was never a requirement for the job." ~ Jay Holmes

While there was certainly plenty of actual activity in Central America to witness, the majority of "witnesses" who spoke to the multitude of journalists hanging out in the cities were willing to say whatever the journalists wanted to hear in exchange for a free meal, a dollar or two, or whatever else was given them for "information." And, of course, there were plenty of "corroborating witnesses" in the form of family and friends. Whatever yarn the journalists wanted to spin was in no short supply of eyewitnessing, and the same witness who said they "saw the Sandinistas slaughter a village" when talking to a journalist at breakfast were likely to tell a different journalist that they "saw the government death squads slaughter a village" that same afternoon.

In short, journalists virtually never found out firsthand what was going on in the jungles, nor did they particularly care to do so. Those journalists who worked for left-leaning newspapers wrote articles blaming all the violence on right-wing factions, and they had plenty of "witnesses" to support their claims. Those journalists who worked for right-leaning newspapers wrote articles blaming all the violence on left-wing factions, and they often had the very same "witnesses" on hand to support *their* claims. Actual witnesses were often drowned out by the chaos or too afraid to speak up. As a result, what finally made it into print was far more revealing of the political leanings of the media outlets than it was about the situation in Central America.

The truth is that Cold War Central America was a cauldron of anarchic violence, endemic corruption, and a complete lack of civil rights under any doctrine or government—left or right. Death squads murdered, and "witnesses" told any tale that would make a buck to journalists who didn't care if the whole thing was a lie as long as they met their deadlines. The oligarchy ruthlessly crushed the poor of the nation, while the Soviets funded rebels in their own Soviet quest to establish themselves on the continents of the Western Hemisphere in the name of the International

Soviet dream. Neighbors turned on neighbors, and brothers turned on brothers. No one was above suspicion. The suffering and injustices weren't caused by left or right, and they could not be fixed by leftism or rightism. The rule of the day was pure bedlam.

One of the most important examples of this chaos was the assassination of Oscar Arnulfo Romero y Galdámez, the fourth archbishop of San Salvador.

ASSASSINATION OF ARCHBISHOP OSCAR ROMERO

Archbishop Romero was, by all reports, a genuinely decent, caring man who no doubt knew he was risking his life to speak out on behalf of the poor population of El Salvador that suffered at the hands of paramilitary right-wing factions and the Revolutionary Government Juntas. As we tell this tale, keep in mind that there are no definitive records from this period of time in El Salvador. Chaos was king. It was a time of military juntas, death squads, Soviet-backed rebels, the CIA fighting the Soviet-backed rebels, reporters all trying to meet deadlines and make a buck—and all of it capped off with the Soviet Union flooding the media with false stories and contradictory accounts for the express purpose of keeping people confused and running in circles. Like we said. C.H.A.O.S.

Archbishop Romero was born in the town of Ciudad Barrios, San Miguel, El Salvador, on August 15, 1917. At the age of thirteen, he entered the minor seminary in San Miguel. He continued his religious studies at the national seminary in San Salvador and went on to graduate from the Gregorian University in Rome. He was ordained in 1942 and, stuck in Italy because of WWII travel restrictions, continued his schooling with the goal of obtaining a doctoral degree in Theology. On his way home to San Salvador via Spain and Cuba in 1943, Father Romero was detained by Cuban police for no apparent reason. Cuba sent him to an internment camp. After several months, he became sick and was sent to a hospital. For reasons as mysterious as the cause for his detention, Romero was released from the hospital and allowed to travel home.

Romero served the people of San Miguel and San Salvador, founding various apostolic groups and Alcoholics Anonymous and assisting in the construction of San Miguel's cathedral. He worked closely with the impoverished people of rural El Salvador and became very conservative in the process. He was a staunch supporter of the traditions of the Catholic Church. In 1974, Romero was appointed Bishop of the Diocese of Santiago de Maria, and in 1977, he became the archbishop of San Salvador.

Three weeks after Romero became archbishop, his close friend, a Jesuit priest by the name of Rutilio Grande, was assassinated. Grande had been working with the poor of El Salvador, creating self-reliance groups. When he was assassinated, the El Salvadoran government refused to investigate, and the government-censored press buried the story. Archbishop Romero was moved and inspired by his friend's murder and vowed to continue Grande's mission. Romero became an activist on the part of the poor, speaking out against torture, assassinations, social injustices, and the practices that perpetuated poverty. The poor loved him. The ruling classes did not.

Violence escalated during this time that would prove to be a prelude to the Salvadoran Civil War. Death squads spawned, priests were attacked and murdered, and three successive Revolutionary Government Juntas comprised of the El Salvadoran oligarchy took charge of the country. Archbishop Romero continued in his advocacy for the poor against the Salvadoran government, charging it with sanctioning terror and assassinations with its death squads. He also sharply criticized the United

States for giving military aid to the Revolutionary Government Juntas. Romero became an international figure.

On March 24, 1980, Archbishop Oscar Romero was killed by a sniper as he was saying mass. His final words were, "May this body immolated and this blood sacrificed for humans nourish us also, so that we may give our body and blood to suffering and to pain—like Christ, not for ourselves, but to teach justice and peace to our people. So let us join together intimately in faith and hope at this moment of prayer for Doña Sarita and for ourselves." He raised the chalice, and the sniper shot him.

Archbishop Romero's funeral was held on March 30, 1980. Well over one hundred thousand mourners attended. Bishops and priests from around the world, journalists, leftist groups, and the poor of El Salvador thronged the plaza and the streets around the Catedral Metropolitana de San Salvador. According to reports from the Catholic officials present, representatives from the El Salvadoran government and members of the El Salvadoran oligarchy were notably missing from the crowd. Also, according to Archbishop John Quinn of San Francisco, who attended the funeral, the Boy Scouts were present. They were in charge of crowd control.

Yes. You heard us correctly. Boy Scouts running crowd control. If indeed they were there—and nothing is certain about that day—it was likely because the Church saw them as a group that the people would respect that wasn't representing either the right-wing oligarchy or the left-wing rebels. We don't know if the Boy Scouts in El Salvador earned a special merit badge for this type of service. Like we keep saying, things and people are different in different parts of the world.

According to Archbishop Quinn, things went well until Cardinal Ernesto Corripio Ahumada of Mexico began to speak. At that point, Quinn reports gunfire and an explosion in the back corner of the plaza, where the leftist groups were gathered.

According to Quinn, Cardinal Corripio attempted to calm the crowd, but another explosion set the masses into a panic. The clergy and approximately five thousand people stampeded into the cathedral and packed up against each other. The room was sweltering, and people began to faint. Outside, bombs and gunfire continued. Periodically, people carried in a corpse and left it by the side wall of the sanctuary. One attacker ran in, looked around, and left without shooting. Reporters snapped pictures and conducted interviews inside the cathedral. Not knowing if or when the attackers would kill those who had taken sanctuary, Archbishop Quinn gave the crowd a general absolution.

The violence lasted for two to three hours. With bombs blasting and bullets flying, Archbishop Romero's casket was laid to rest in the tomb. Cardinal Corripio said the burial prayers, and the tomb was closed. Reports of the dead and injured vary, but we believe it is safe to say that approximately thirty people were killed during the attack. Whether or not the violence at Archbishop Romero's funeral was organized by the same people responsible for his assassination is something we will likely never know.

Archbishop Romero is still an important figure in Latin American societies and in the Catholic Church. In 1990, Pope John Paul II began the process of beatification and eventual canonization of Archbishop Romero. In 1997, Romero was given the title "Servant of God," and the pope commemorated him as a martyr on May 7, 2000. Archbishop Romero was beatified on May 23, 2014.

Numerous theories abound about who killed Archbishop Oscar Romero. No one knows for certain to this day as to which, if any, are correct.

The most popular theory is that Romero was killed by a right-wing death squad that had been organized by Salvadoran leader Roberto D'Aubuisson on behalf of the Salvadoran oligarchs. The first thing to understand about that theory is that the oligarchs of El Salvador did not act as one body. At the time of Romero's assassination, the Salvadoran government was run by the third Revolutionary Government Junta that had taken charge in the past year. The Salvadoran government was in pandemonium. Dictators were in place, but they didn't necessarily have control of the military, police, or the other wealthy citizens of El Salvador. There were people in the oligarchy capable of murdering Oscar Romero without the president and his cabinet being complicit. D'Aubuisson had motive, but so did many others among the right-wing oligarchy.

Numerous witnesses report that D'Aubuisson ordered Archbishop Romero's assassination, which brings us to the next thing to consider with the theory. As we mentioned above, witnesses came cheap in El Salvador in the 1980s. This highlights a problem with intelligence in general...

"When you've got the cash and the 'witnesses' don't, some of those 'witnesses' will say anything they think you want to hear to get the money." ~ Jay Holmes

There are interviews with men who said they were actually on D'Auboisson's death squad and present the day of the assassination. Again, as we mentioned above, those same witnesses might have spun a completely different tale for the next person who held out cash.

Another thing to consider with the theory that Romero was assassinated by right-wing death squads is that the right wing tended to be Catholic and conservative. Although Romero had angered the right-wing oligarchy with his denunciation of their oppression of the poor, the individuals in the right-wing death squads were unlikely to be comfortable with the idea of assassinating a Catholic archbishop or murdering his faithful followers at his very Catholic funeral.

If it *was* the right-wing oligarchy that had Romero killed, then the move backfired. Few Americans or Europeans had heard of Archbishop Romero before he was assassinated. After his assassination and the ensuing slaughter at his funeral, Americans and Europeans became aware of Romero and his message about the oligarch's oppression of the people of El Salvador. He was an overnight martyr and representative of the injustices being perpetrated in Central America. Because of this new international awareness, it became more difficult for the anticommunist oligarchs of El Salvador to obtain support from the United States.

We know what you're thinking . . . Wait! What? How could the United States give aid to these dirtbags?

At the time, America's imperative interest was in keeping the Soviet Union from expanding its influence and power deeper into the Western Hemisphere. Americans did not yet suffer under the weight of the idea that America should be the World Police, or that every dysfunctional country was only one despotic dictator's overthrow away from Utopia. The United States had come out of WWII to find itself in a power struggle with the Soviet Empire, whose stated mission was to convert the entire planet to Soviet-style communism. The imperative mission of our presidents and of our foreign policy was to defend against the advances of the Soviet Union and other communist countries. That is what the United States did. In Central America, the US government saw the anticommunist oligarchs as the lesser of evils *for the United States* as compared to the Soviet-backed rebels. And so the US gave aid to the oligarchs.

Another theory about the assassination of Archbishop Romero is that a leftist death squad killed him in order to have a martyr for their movement. If that was the case, that group may or may not have been directly under the control of Cuba or Moscow. That doesn't mean that the Politburo didn't know about it, mull it over, and give the go-ahead. It just means that the group could have been working independently of any governmental direction. That happened frequently. As we pointed out above, death squads were not the coordinated, government-directed forces the media made them out to be, whether they were right wing or left wing.

That being said, if there was left-wing involvement in the assassination of Archbishop Romero, it was likely that the Soviets *were* behind it. It was common for the Soviets to murder left-wing socialist leaders.

So why would the Soviets murder the very people who were advocating for socialist and communist regimes and making inroads for Soviet influence?

The Soviet Union's mission was to make the entire world Soviet communists. The Soviets always saw Russia as the base and capital of an International Soviet Union, and they sought followers in other countries who would be loyal to the idea of the "International Soviet." The last thing the Soviets wanted in any of the countries they targeted was genuine social justice warriors who were fighting for the good of the people rather than for the International Soviet vision, and those SJWs were the "useful idiots"—as the Soviets called them—that the Soviets always purged first when they took charge of a country. Those SJWs were frequently martyred by the Soviets because "useful dead idiots" were often more useful to them than "useful live idiots." It was common for Soviet-controlled agents and personnel to whack a leftist and flood the market with outrage propaganda that the right-wingers had committed the assassination.

Leaders like Archbishop Romero were not interested in being the International Soviet. Romero's mission was not to spread Soviet communism. His mission was to bring justice to the impoverished people of El Salvador. The Soviet Union, on the other hand, rather specialized at expanding poverty and dishing out injustice to impoverished people. (Just ask Cuba.) That means Romero would have been just as much of an activist against any actual Soviet-led communist regime in El Salvador as he was against the oligarchs. Alive, he was going to make trouble. Dead, he was an international martyr for the communist cause and a strike point against the Salvadoran anticommunist regimes. *Much more useful to Moscow dead.*

And, of course, there is the old standby theory whenever mystery shrouds an assassination anywhere on the planet—that the CIA did it. *yawn* As we point out above, the death squads were anathema to the CIA's mission in Central America. Such assassinations and the massacres of innocents only fueled the communist movements, and the US knew that.

Chaos was the word of the day, assassins and witnesses were easily bought, and today's death-squad leaders were tomorrow's public officials. Both the oligarchs and the leftist rebels had reason to see Romero dead. Add to that the fact that the Soviets exploited the situation whether they caused it or not by flooding the market with conflicting stories and outrage against right-wingers. What we're left with is one hard fact—that we will likely never know the truth of who was behind the trigger pull that killed Archbishop Romero. The only matter for certain is that a good man was murdered.

Archbishop Romero's assassination is only one example of the rampant turmoil and brutality of the death squads of Central

America. As we said, these activities only hurt the US mission to keep the Soviets from expanding their influence in the Western Hemisphere. As a response to the brutality, the United States established the US Army's School of the Americas ("SOA") in Fort Benning, Georgia. The media and popular culture have widely portrayed the SOA as a training ground for vicious assassins. In reality, the US Department of Defense and the US Army were trying to train the governments of our Central American allies and their military and police personnel to be *less* ruthless and more selective in their use of violence so they did not drive citizens into the arms of the Soviets.

It is true that many graduates of the SOA, such as Roberto D'Auboisson, went on to be involved in horrible corruption and violence against their own people, but those were *not* things that they learned at the SOA. The staff of SOA has always understood that massacres of villages of innocent people help drive rebellions and do not bring security to the establishment. For stability, governments must restrict their violence to people they know are guilty of major crimes and not just people who are suspected of association with communists.

In September of 1993, Congress took up the debate over the SOA and tried to defund it. Many congressmen, such as Senator Teddy Kennedy, were convinced America was training Central Americans to be violent. However, since violence in Central America was not invented by the US Army, the CIA, or the Department of Defense, closing the SOA would have done nothing to reduce the violence in that region.

Nevertheless, the SOA was closed in 2001, and a successor institution was founded, the Western Hemisphere Institute for Security Cooperation ("WHINSEC"). While at least one former SOA teacher reports that the classes are still the same, researcher Ruth Blakeley states in the book *Critical Approaches to Security: An Intro-*

duction to Theories and Methods that at WHINSEC, ". . . a much more rigorous human rights training program was in place than in any other US military institution."

Bottom Line: Central America in the 1970s and 1980s was a hotbed of chaotic violence, and the death squads only made it harder for the United States to fulfill its own mission of keeping Soviet influence out of the Western hemisphere.

Writing Tip: When writing about regions in the throes of revolution, you *cannot* overplay the chaos, violence, conspiracies, profiteering, and corruption, but you *can* realistically write great souls who rise above it.

27
WHEN GOOD MISSIONS GO BAD—THE EXIT STRATEGY

"It's hard to maintain your cover after killing the locals." ~ Jay Holmes

SOMETIMES GOOD SPOOKS HAVE BAD DAYS. COVERS GET BLOWN. Things get loud. Bodies pile up. Then what happens? The answer to that varies with each mission and each situation, but the thing to know every time is that the saying "time is precious" is never more true than in that moment. Whatever move a spook makes must be made quickly.

The main factor that impacts a spook in that critical moment is whether or not they are in a "denied area," meaning a hostile country such as Russia, China, Iran, Cuba, etc., or generally a location where foreigners can't routinely walk around, as they can, say, in France. If a spook is *not* in a denied area, their main concerns will be not getting caught and not embarrassing their own country. They likely don't need to worry that they or any of their assets will be tortured or killed. On the other hand, if a spook *is* operating in a denied area when their cover is blown, it could cause an international incident, and not only they, but any assets or associates could be tortured and killed if they are caught. Whether or not a spook is in a denied area will determine their resources and their course of action.

A good spook has a fallout plan going into the mission, particularly if that mission is in a denied area. The options for that plan change with each situation, but going out on a dangerous mission with no backup plan and no plan for what happens if trouble starts is living dangerously, indeed.

The two most important parts of a fallout plan are "where" and "when." The "where" is all about getting the hell out of Dodge, especially when a spook is in a denied area. This will include having some method of transportation in place to get *away* from wherever they are and to get *to* someplace with connections to get out of the country. The "when" is about knowing *when* to get the hell out of Dodge. If a spook jumps too soon, they could blow an otherwise viable mission. If they jump too late, they could be captured, tortured, and/or killed. With most people in covert activity, one of the toughest things to train them to do is to pay attention to the signs that a mission is going bad and to back out.

Sometimes a spook needs more than one backup plan, and the plan they use will depend on how far the mission has progressed. For example, a spook could be in different places at different times in the operation. They could also be dealing with different groups of people at different times. Different locations and different groups mean different plans. In other words, the backup plans have backup plans.

One of the most important things about backup plans for a spook is working with people upon whom they can trust and rely. This is often when support personnel come in handy.

Support personnel are those who are already stationed in a foreign country under a legend. Their job is to be on hand to assist transient operators or teams by delivering supplies, bribing them out of jail, helping them escape the country, or in any other way they can. They work alone, and their legend could include a day job that is anything from a cosmetics company employee to a dock worker to a banker—any unremarkable position for a foreigner to hold. The support personnel may or may not be able to trust the local American embassy personnel, and they may or may not be under surveillance by any number of people at any given time. It is one of the loneliest and most psychologically difficult jobs in the field, and few people do it more than three years max. A good support person can have one or more fallout plans in place for a spook before the spook arrives, and they can be critical to a field spook's survival when good missions go bad.

"The quality of the people is just as important as the quality of the plan." ~ Jay Holmes

Writing Tip: Create a protagonist who is support personnel to other spooks coming through a hostile country. There would be no end to the danger, the variety of tasks, or the colorful personalities with whom they would deal, not to mention the psychological issues that would wear them down.

28

THE HARDEST PART OF THE MISSION

ONE MIGHT THINK THE MOST DIFFICULT PART OF THE MISSION MIGHT be keeping calm while rolling a snatched target out of a building in a wheelchair behind enemy lines, or the physical exertion of skydiving out of an airplane into the ocean and scuba diving up to shore to blow up an enemy compound. While those are certainly trying, and some would say invigorating, they are not the most psychologically difficult parts of a mission. That part comes early on when the spook transitions from being a normal, everyday person with loved ones and a name their mother knows to becoming the legend. That transition is marked by giving up their wallet.

For all intents and purposes, a spook is abandoning their family and loved ones while on the mission. Sometimes a spouse *might* have a contact number for extreme emergencies. Some spouses never even have that—just a rough estimate of when their beloved will return, and that estimate is often inaccurate.

As discussed in the chapter on The Spook Reality, it is difficult, but unavoidable, that certain factors make it an extreme security risk for spouses of some spooks to know anything about the spook's mission. Such knowledge would turn a spouse and even an entire family into targets. Enemies could kidnap and torture them for information. If our enemies are reasonably certain that this variety of spooks never tell their spouses or families anything, there is no point in our enemies going after their families. The other unavoidable factor is that few marriages survive the spook's lifestyle, and spouses can be vindictive. They can either sell information or use it to help our enemies find their exes. As a result, a spouse must be as committed to the mission as the spook is, and they must live that commitment by refraining from asking questions or expecting any information.

When a spook turns over their wallet with their ID, library cards, credit cards, laundry receipts, and, most importantly, pictures of their loved ones, they may experience a sharp pang of guilt and say a prayer for the people they are leaving behind. In that act, they consciously place the greater good over their own and that of their families. They know that what they are doing could hurt their loved ones, either because they will not be there for their family if something happens at home while they are away, or because they might never come home again. It is heart-wrenching.

Because of this, the moment a spook gets their wallet back is just as pivotal. When they once more have their wallet and its contents in hand, it's like getting a life back. Loved ones are once more available to the spook, and the spook is once more available to them. They might well experience a deep relief and comfort at being reunited with their wallet and their life, even if they aren't actually back with their people yet.

Hollywood loves to write spooks who don't dare love anyone. While it's true that many do not have their own families, it's not because they can't love. On the contrary, many spooks love intensely, and they are so committed to their work because they are farsighted and willing to sacrifice their lives to make the world a better and safer place for those they love.

> **Bottom Line:** Spooks love, and the hardest part of any mission for a deep cover spook is the fact that they must temporarily abandon their loved ones for the sake of the mission.

29

WHAT WILL BE THE NEXT HOT SPOT?

THIS IS A COMMON QUESTION WE GET. OBVIOUSLY, THE MIDDLE East is a perpetual hot spot, and we don't mean because of the desert. As for the "next" hot spot, it's actually a previous hot spot, and it's the Malacca Strait and/or anyplace that is a choke point for energy or natural resources. Every drop of oil going to China from the Middle East passes through the Malacca Strait between Malaysia and Sumatra. It is China's Achilles' heel.

There are plenty of hot spots all the time. Some get hotter or cooler based on what the leadership in various countries decides to do. There aren't actually that many cold spots. If you find one, let us know. We could stand to experience that safe space thing that millennials are always going on about.

30

THE GREATEST MYTH

HOLLYWOOD AND THE PUBLISHING WORLD LOVE TO INDULGE IN angst. Happy characters don't keep people turning the pages or shelling out for movies. However, the entertainment industry's lack of personal experience is never more evident than in how they spin what we call The Angst of the Assassin. In other words, the entertainment industry creates entire movies and books about field spooks that are shattered by regret over killing bad guys instead of giving them candy bars and rehab or simply respecting their right to be bad guys as part of their cultural diversity. Nothing could be further from the truth.

Each and every American field spook is committed not just to keeping our country safe, but to keeping innocents safe. They don't need to be brainwashed to hunt down threats, and it doesn't crush their souls to take out the enemy.

Keep in mind that some field spooks see the worst that humanity has to offer. They know what shattered bodies lie beneath heaps of rubble in bombed-out buildings, and they have viewed the mountains of carcasses dumped into mass graves. They forever see the hollow eyes of children in shock from watching their mothers raped to death and their fathers butchered. They forever hear the primal screams of children burning alive in the fires of terrorist bombs. Any day a spook can take out a bin Laden is a good day, and the overriding feeling when they do so is neither angst nor triumph. It is relief . . . Relief that there is one less evil bastard in the world. A field spook's nightmares are not crowded with the faces of the bad guys they have killed. A field spook's nightmares are teeming with the broken bodies, the haunted eyes, and the visceral screams of the innocents they could not save. When they are able to kill a bin Laden or a Carlos the Jackal, at least for a night or two, they sleep a little bit better.

Indeed, whether we know it or not, we *all* sleep a little bit better.

IN CONCLUSION

This is only a tiny slice of the Shadow World, its people, its history, and its methods. We hope we have communicated the complexities of this world where nothing is constant except change—a world where friends, coworkers, and even lovers can turn out to be deadly enemies. It is known to spooks as the Great Hall of Mirrors for good reason—it is a world wherein true trust is the rarest and highest bond.

We hope we have cleared up some of the murky waters around intelligence organizations, their personnel, and their missions. We hope our efforts help writers see and convey this Shadow World more accurately in fiction as a way of honoring those who live its dangers and sacrifices every day in the world of the real. And we hope that this book, rather than answering all of your questions, causes you to ask questions—of every news report, every political speech, every public official, every seemingly well-meaning social justice cause, and even every friend and neighbor—because the true core of intelligence is understanding that we will never know all there is to know.

And, in closing, we hope we have communicated the essence of why we do what we do—why Holmes and thousands of others have dedicated their lives to keeping the fight from our shores, and why Piper has dedicated her career to writing about that fight in truth and in fiction ... Because we hope. Because we want to share that hope with you.

PHOTO GALLERY

You can find a photo gallery with more illustrations of the Ramzi Yousef Reward Matchbook, Joe Pistone, Herbert O. Yardley, the "Ellis" Dead Drop at Foxstone Park and more at BayardandHolmes.com.

KEY FIGURES IN ESPIONAGE
THE GOOD, THE BAD, & THE BOOTY

With the voice of forty-five years in the Intelligence Community, Bayard & Holmes explore the lives of the espionage elite.

- A one-legged woman operating behind Nazi lines, deemed to be "the most dangerous spy in all of France."
- A young man left for dead, not worth a Viet Cong bullet, who survives to fight terrorists for six more decades.
- A homeless child who becomes an iconic showgirl, entertaining world leaders while running spy rings from the top stages of Europe.
- A traitor operating at the top of Western intelligence whose betrayals caused the deaths of thousands.

More heroic and more treacherous than any fiction Hollywood could produce are these genuine operatives of the Shadow World, who prove that "we're only human" is not an excuse to fail, but a reason to succeed.

Available at BayardandHolmes.com/nonfiction.

ACKNOWLEDGMENTS

Our deepest gratitude to Vicki Hinze, Julee Schwartzburg, Kristen Lamb, and Doug Patteson for production assistance in the publishing of this work.

Our humble indebtedness to our families for their tolerance of our late-night conversations and absenteeism to collaborate on this project.

Our abiding thanks to all of the dedicated professionals who gave us their time and efforts in the review and editing process.

And our undying appreciation to our readers. You make our efforts worthwhile.

Thank you, one and all.